The Art of
THE GREAT
KELDORIAN
DARE

By

S.C. Shuman

Dear reader

On the following pages you will find a lot of the artwork I did while writing THE GREAT KELDORIAN DARE, some illustrating creatures and events that I did not include in the story. I thought some readers might like to see the artwork closer to the full size of the original drawings, even if I did not decide in the end to include them in the story. All of them were done in pencil and then scanned into Photoshop and adjusted there for the final book formatting and printing. I've included the names of the creatures and where they had an actual name (like you and I have), I've included that also. In some cases there is a brief bit of further information on the creature in the drawing to help "place" them in the story narrative.

I hope you enjoy.

Steve Shuman
Cornflakes3591@gmail.com

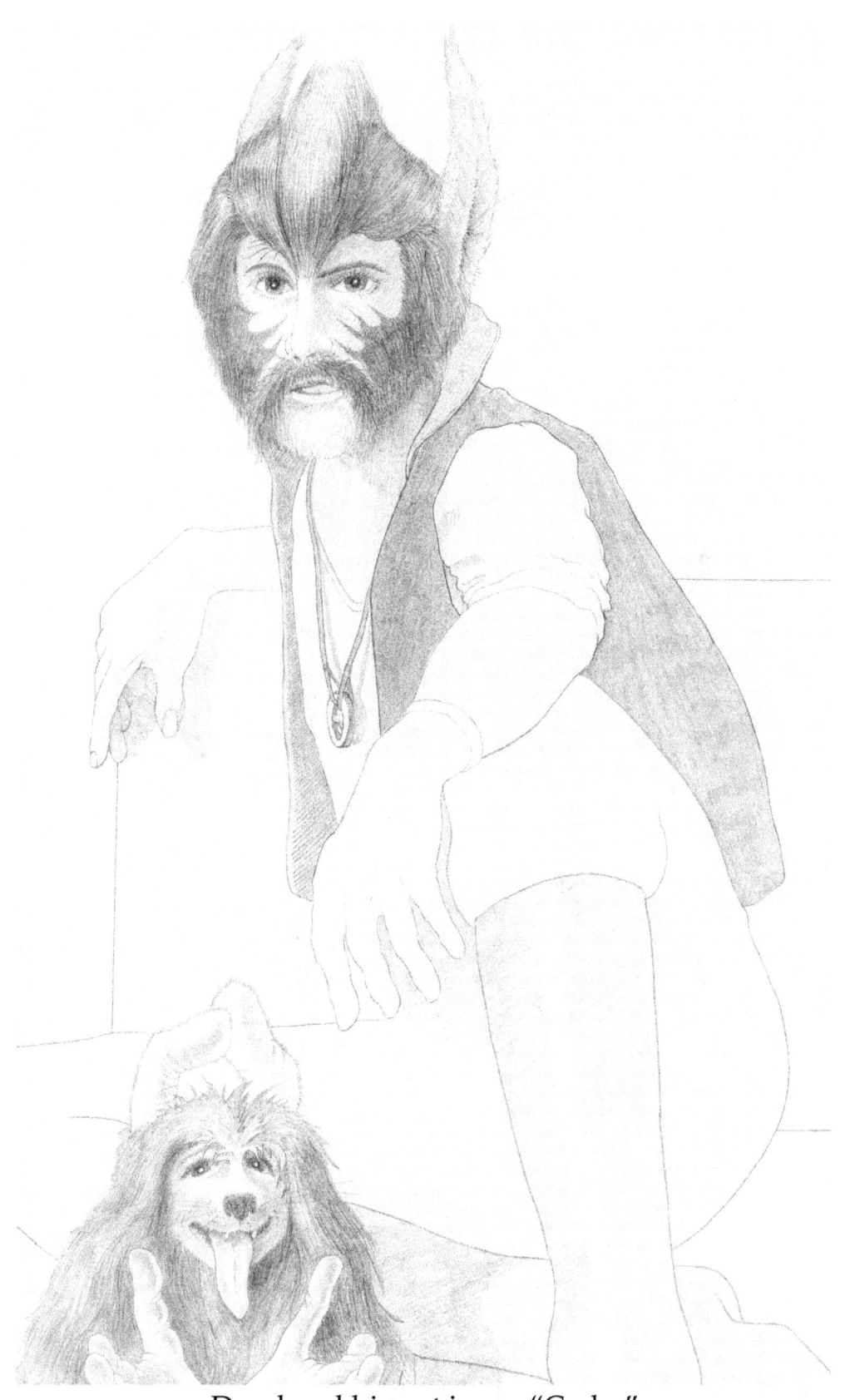

Derol and his pet janga "Carby"

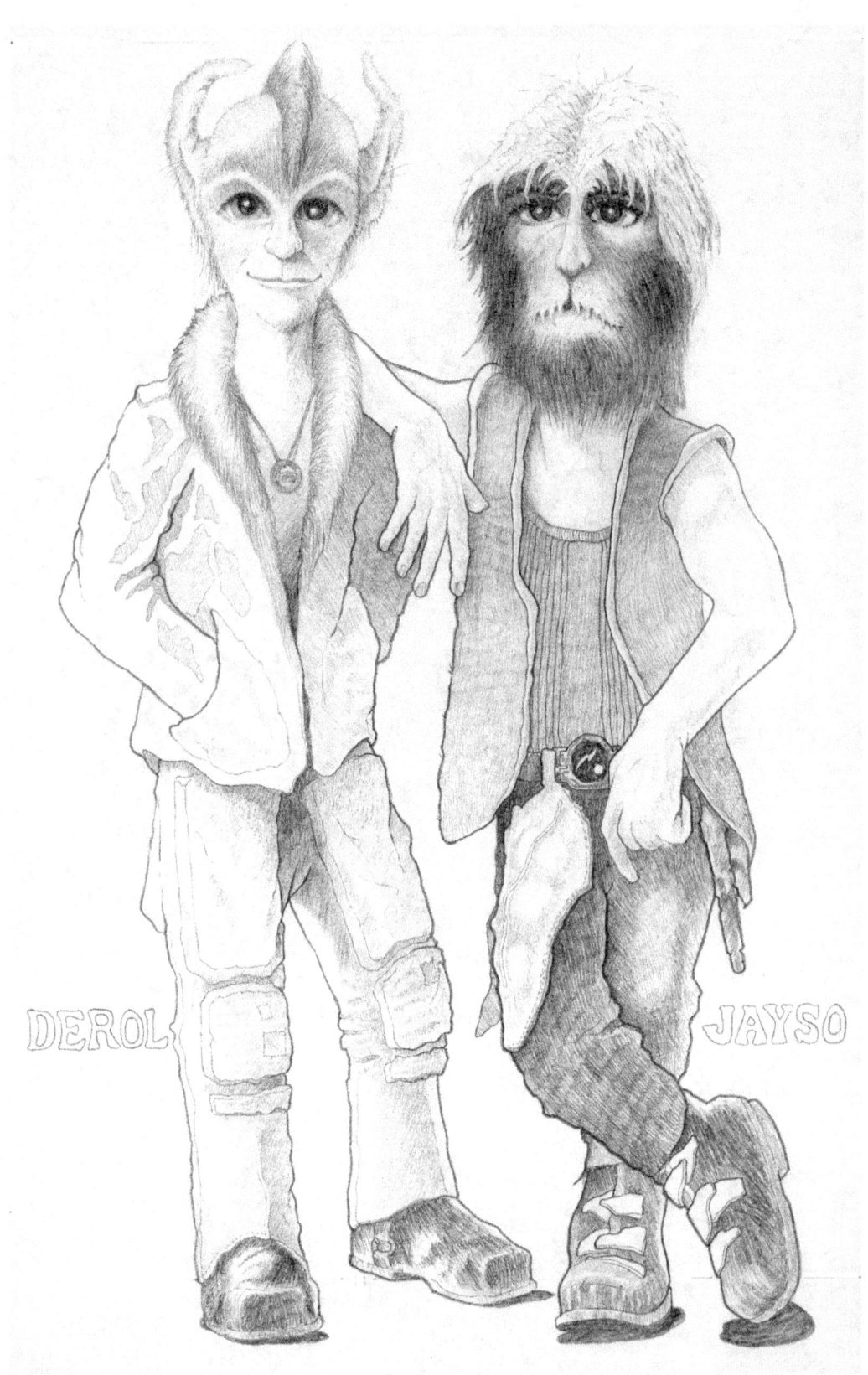

Derol and Jayso in the young early years (not in story)

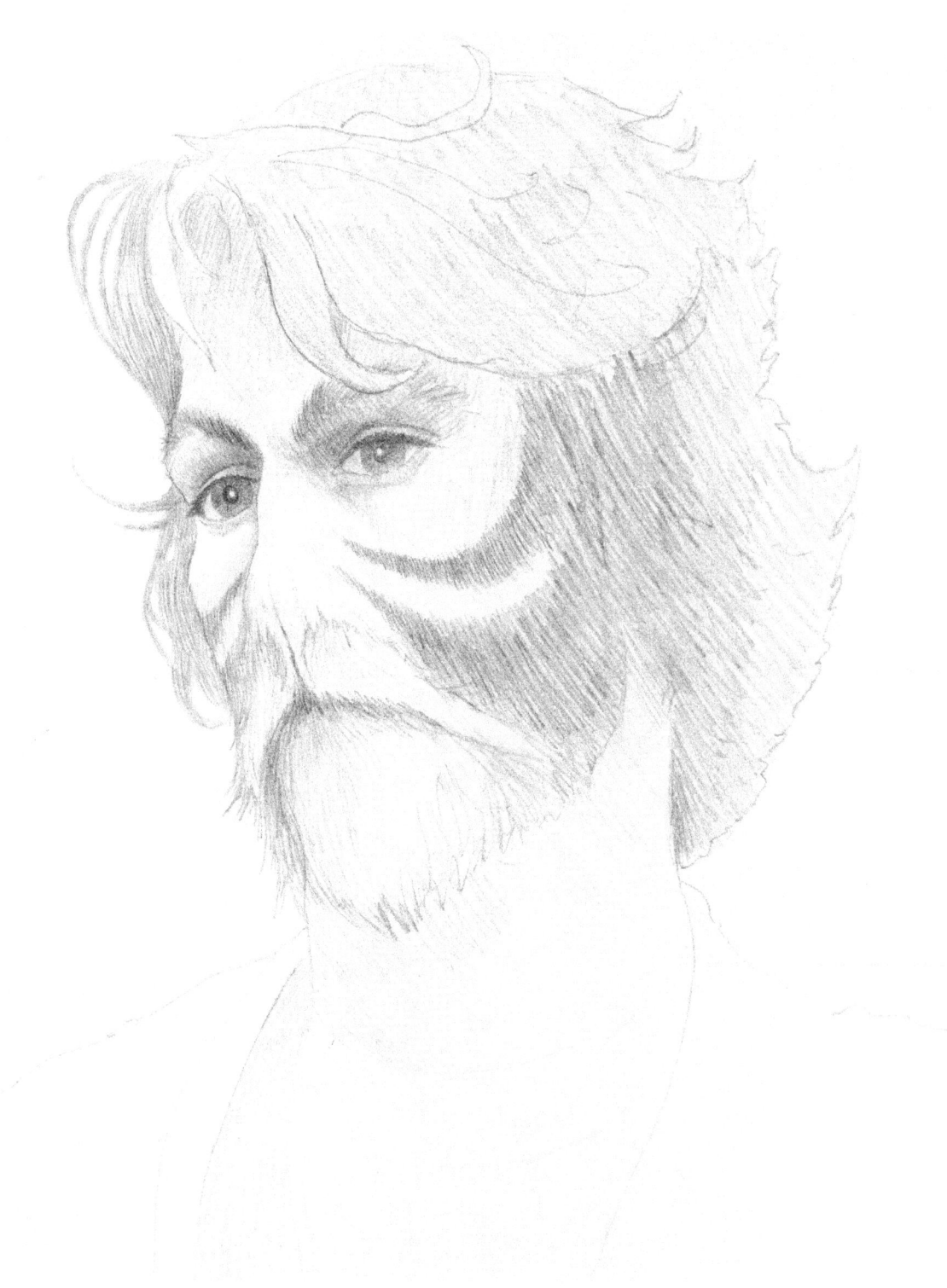

Jayso

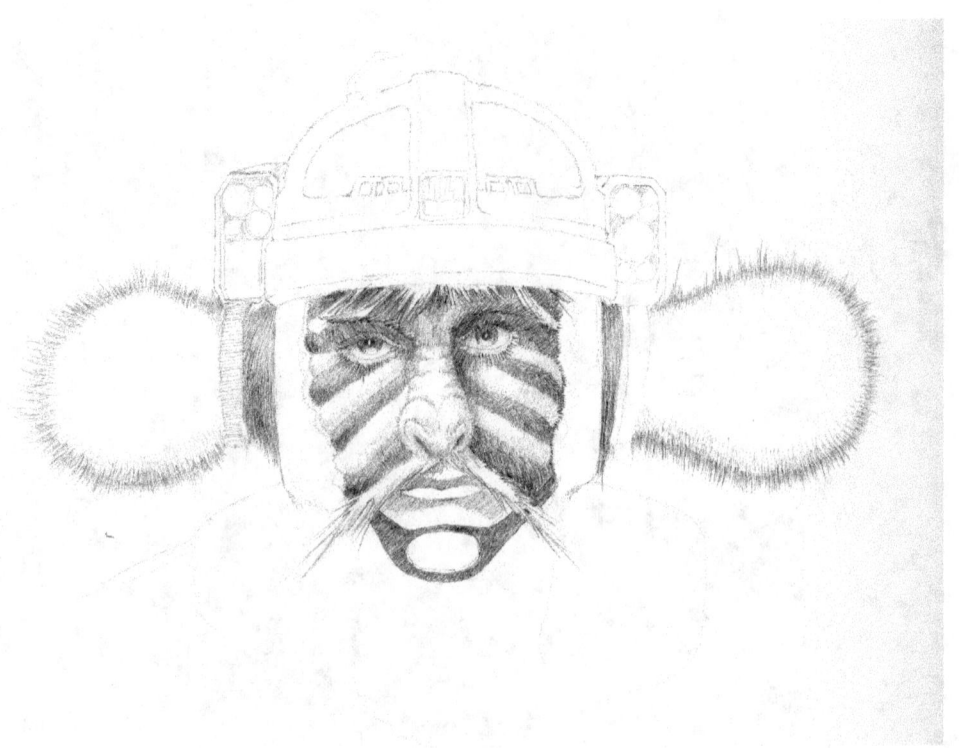

Boge

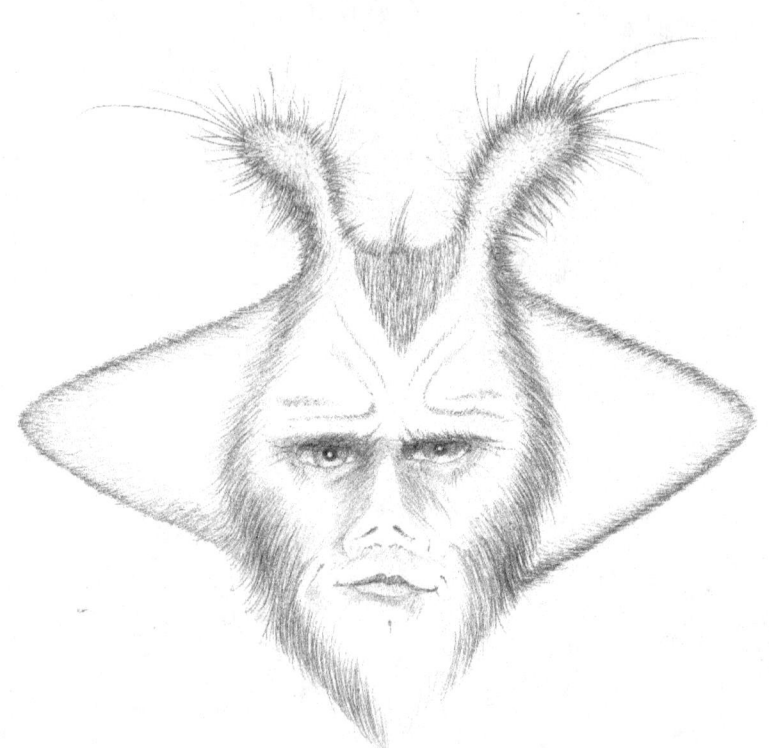

Towder

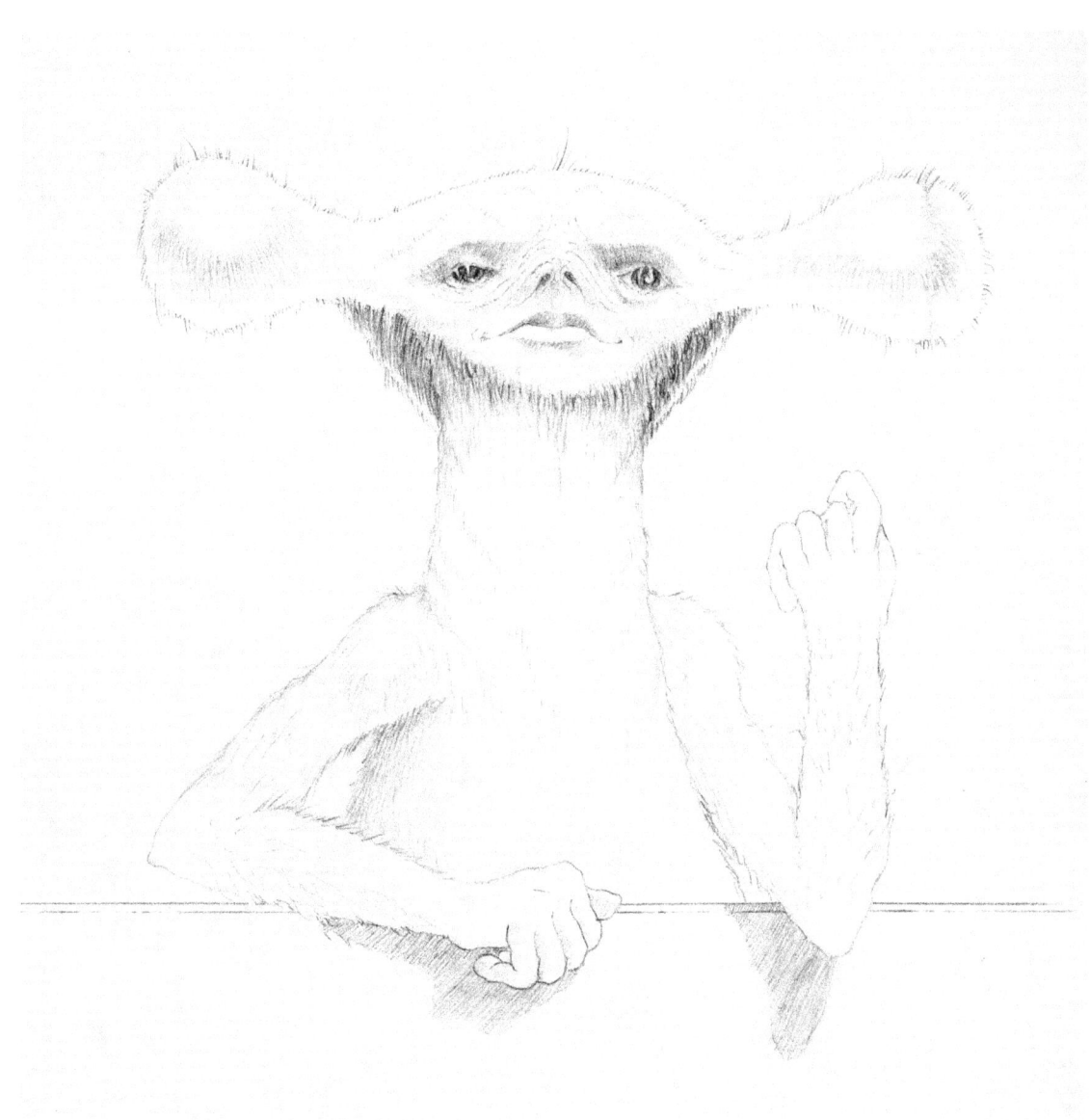

Boge's mother (not in story)

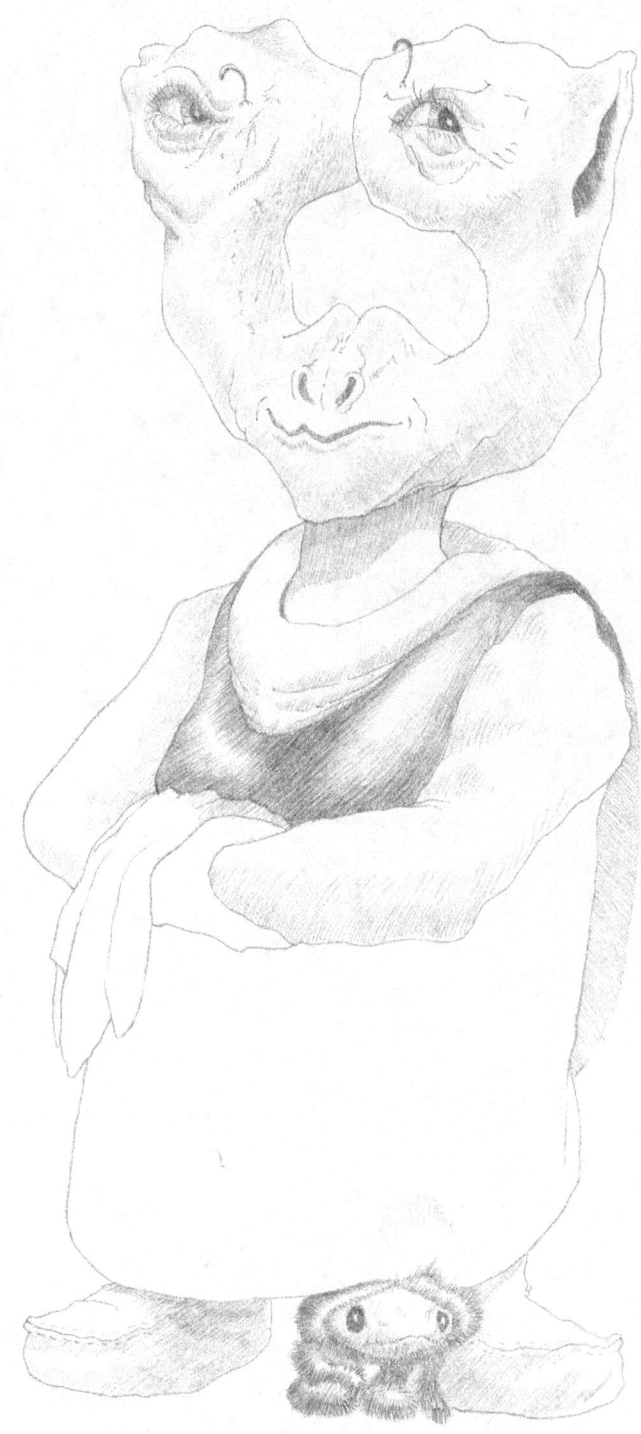

Hibet and her pet whissett

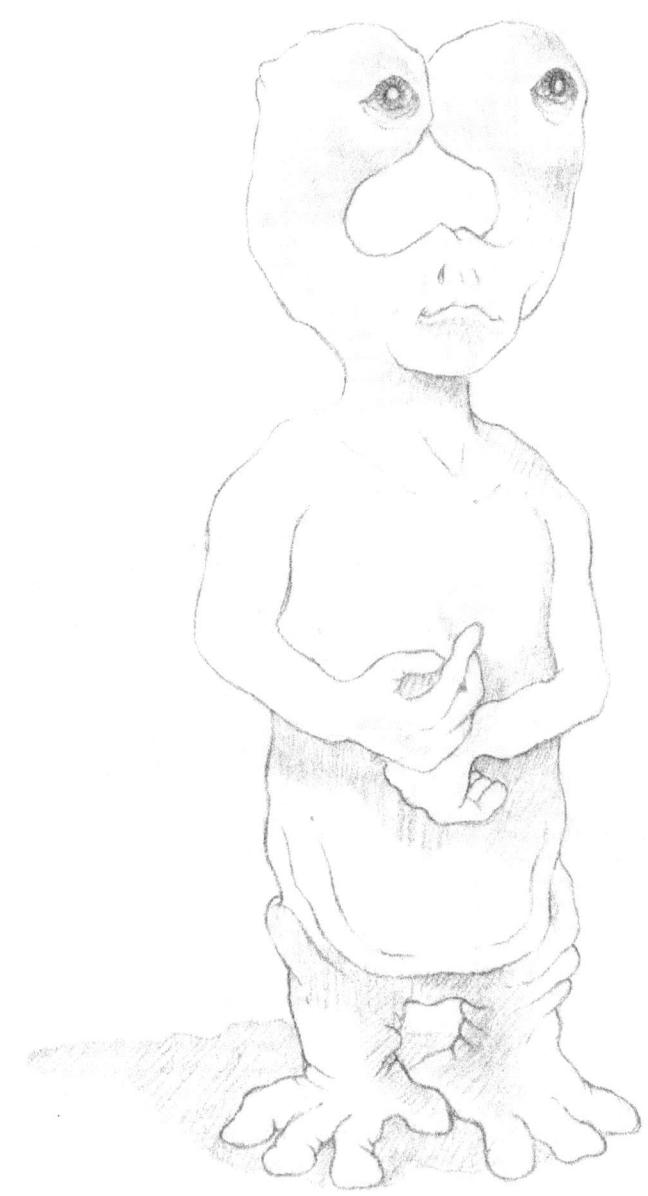

young Hibet

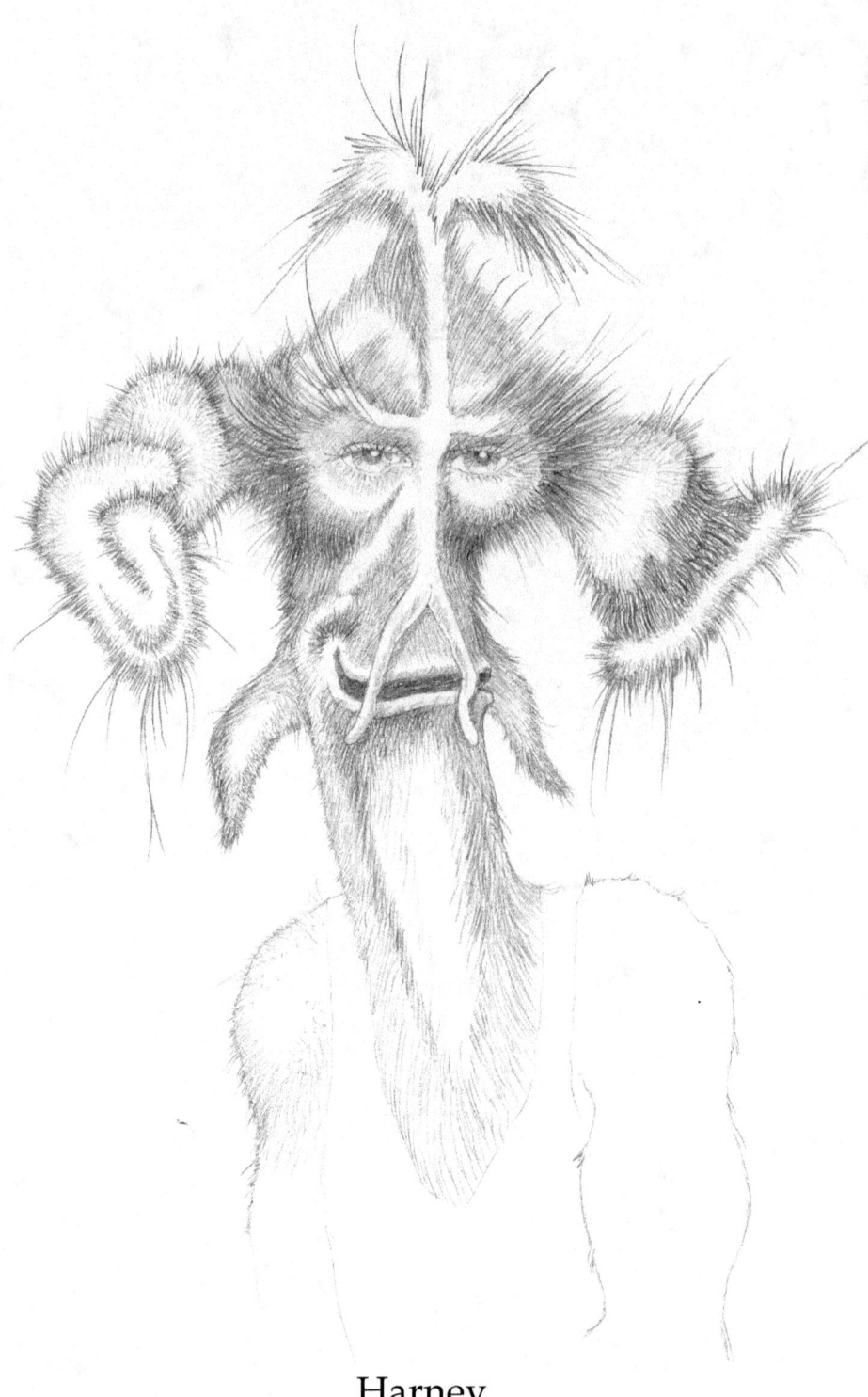

Harney

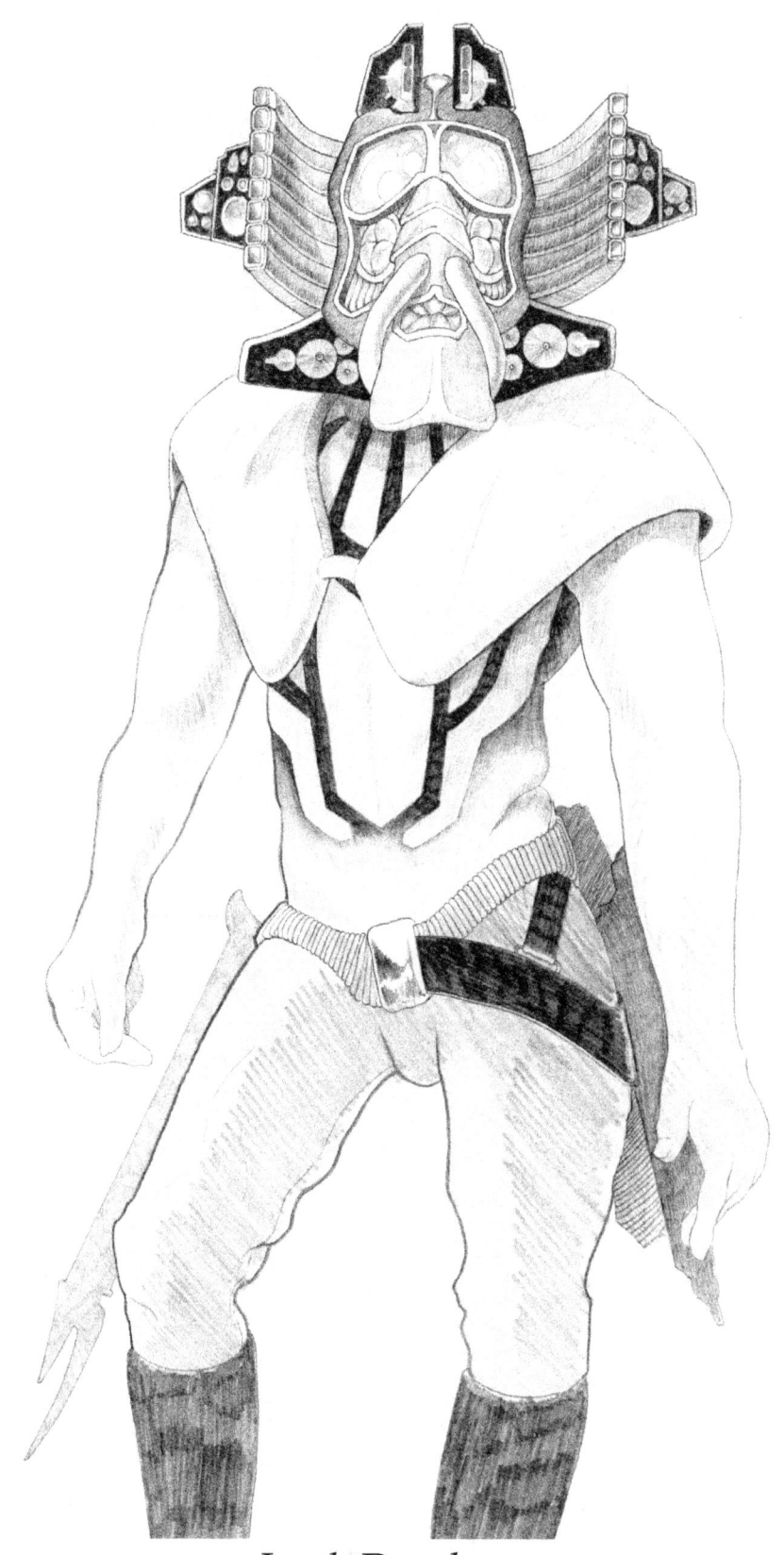

Jooth Doorbon

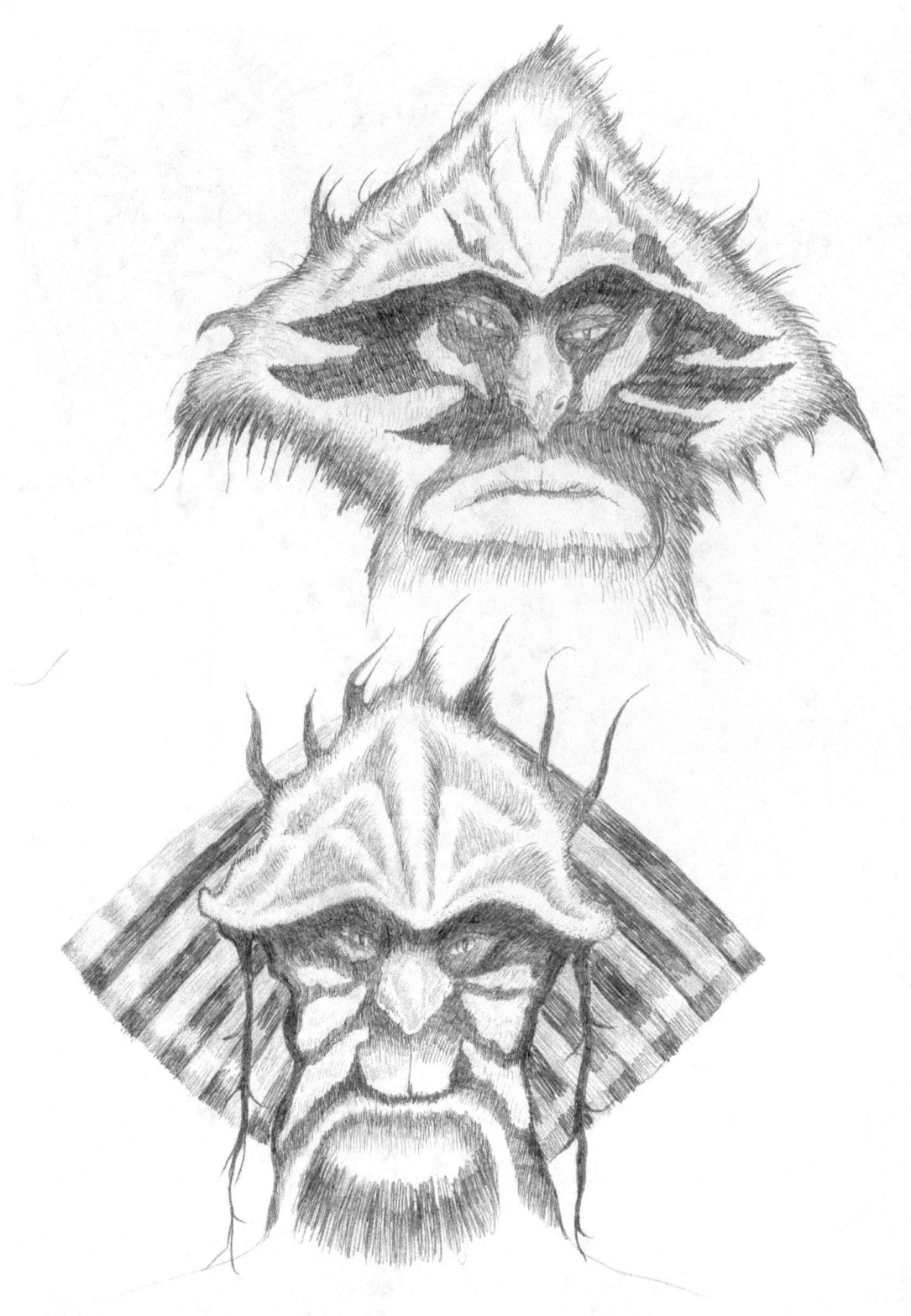

Helmsman on Jooth's spacecruiser (top) and Jooth Doorbon
(without helmet)

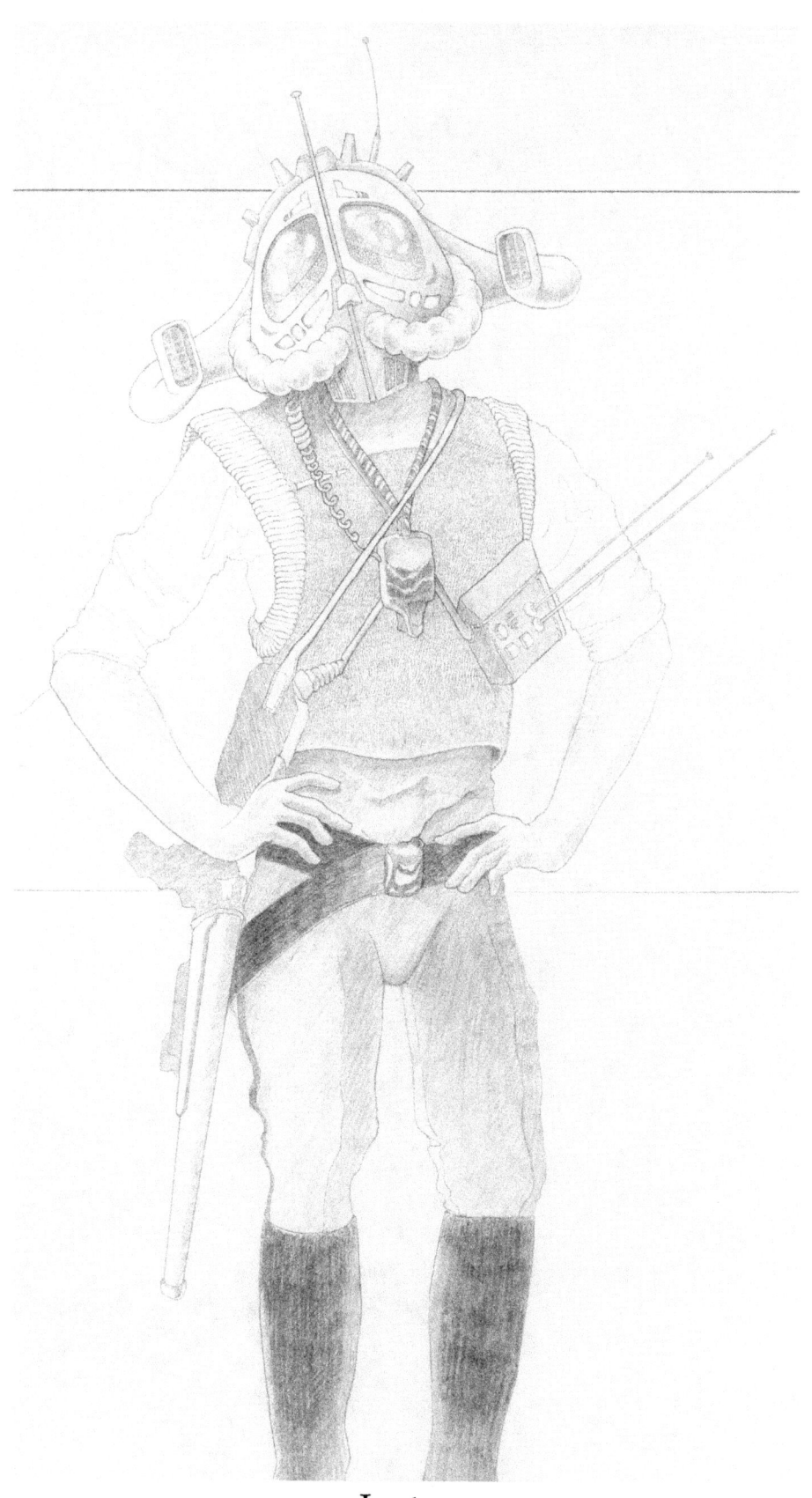

Jaxtor

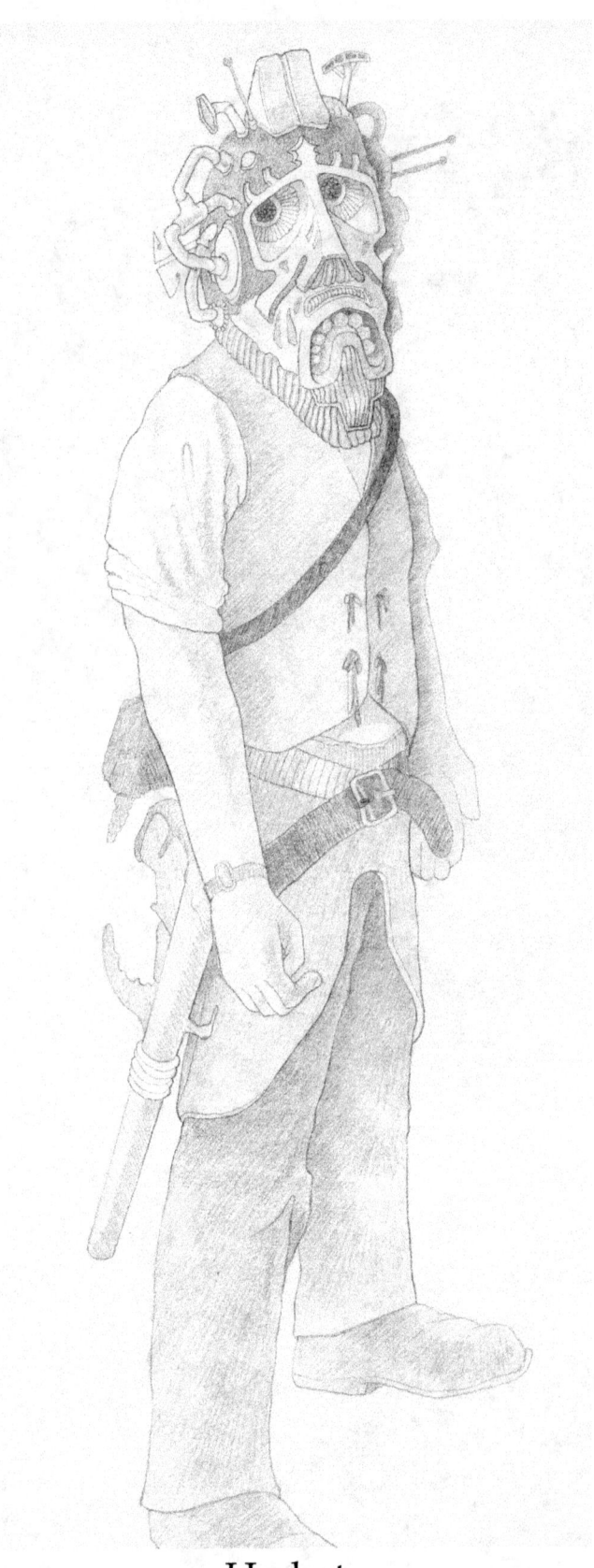

Harbot

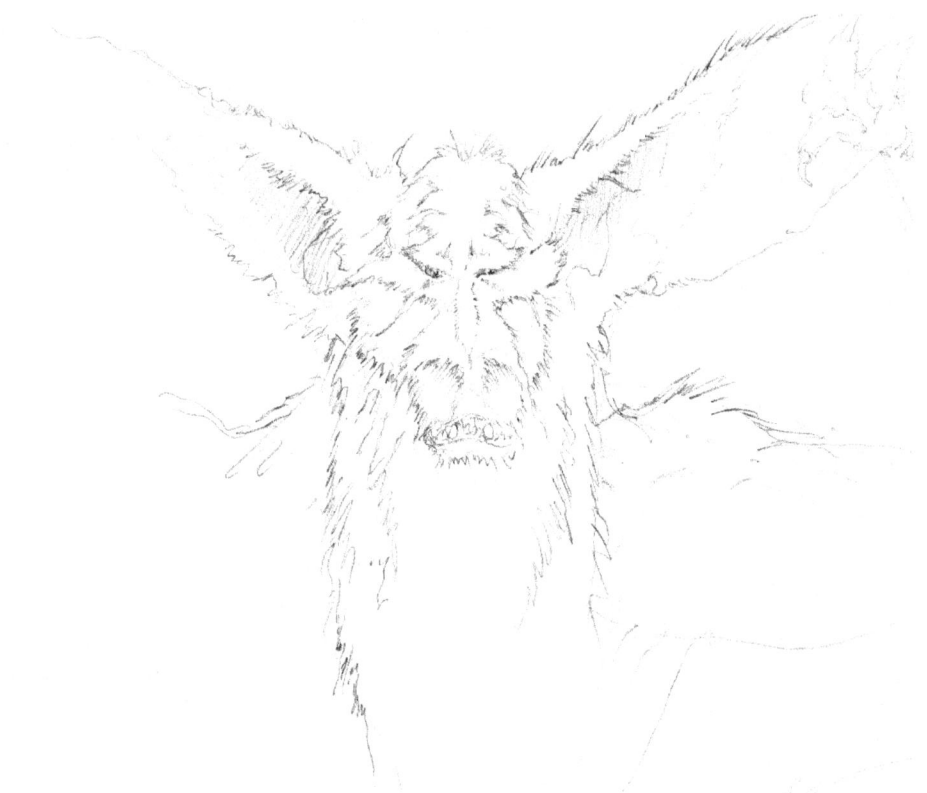

a top level leader in the Delcery Faucord (not in story)

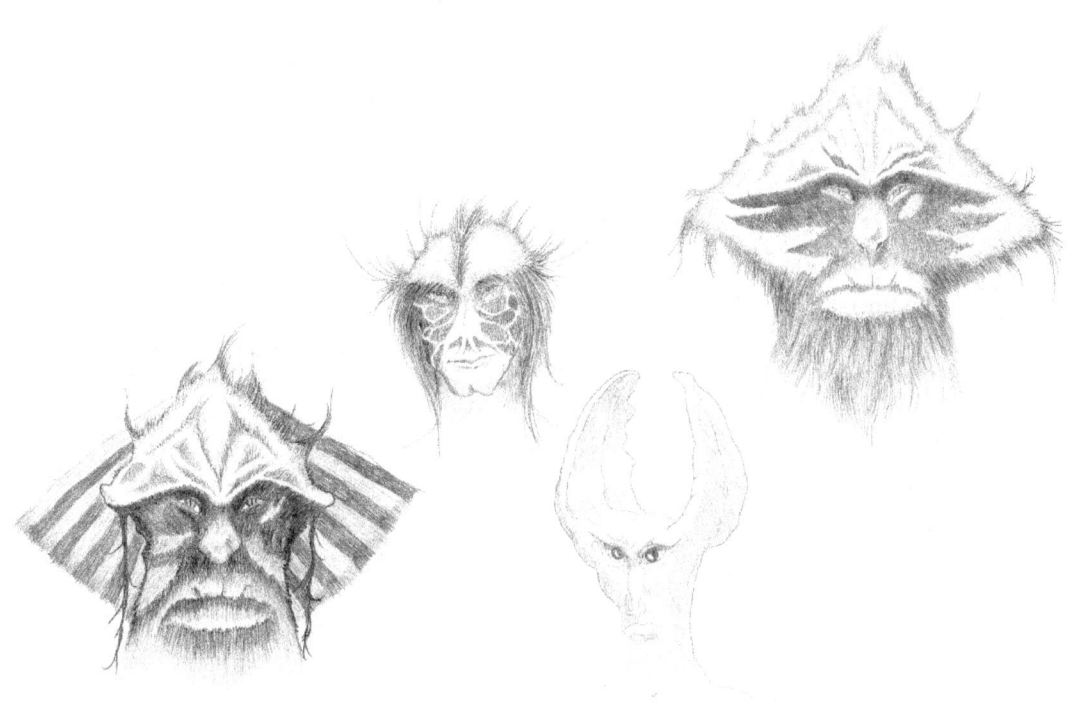

Jooth and some of his friends

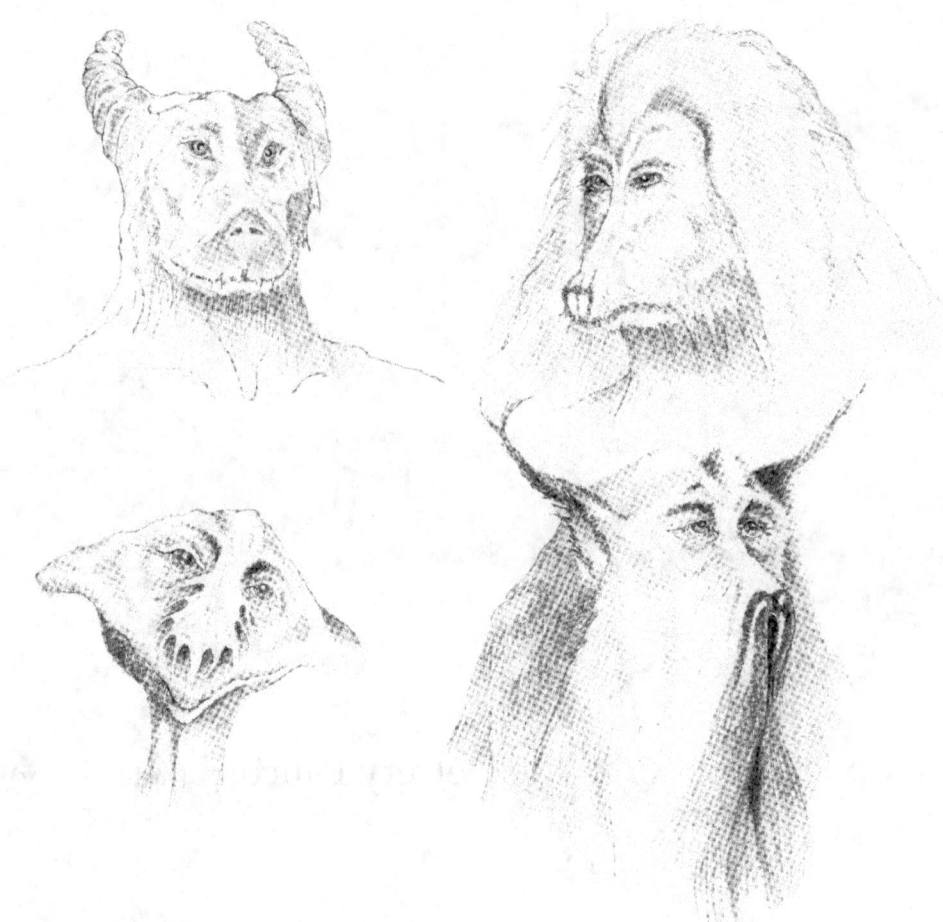

Some of the Delcery Faucord members (not in story)

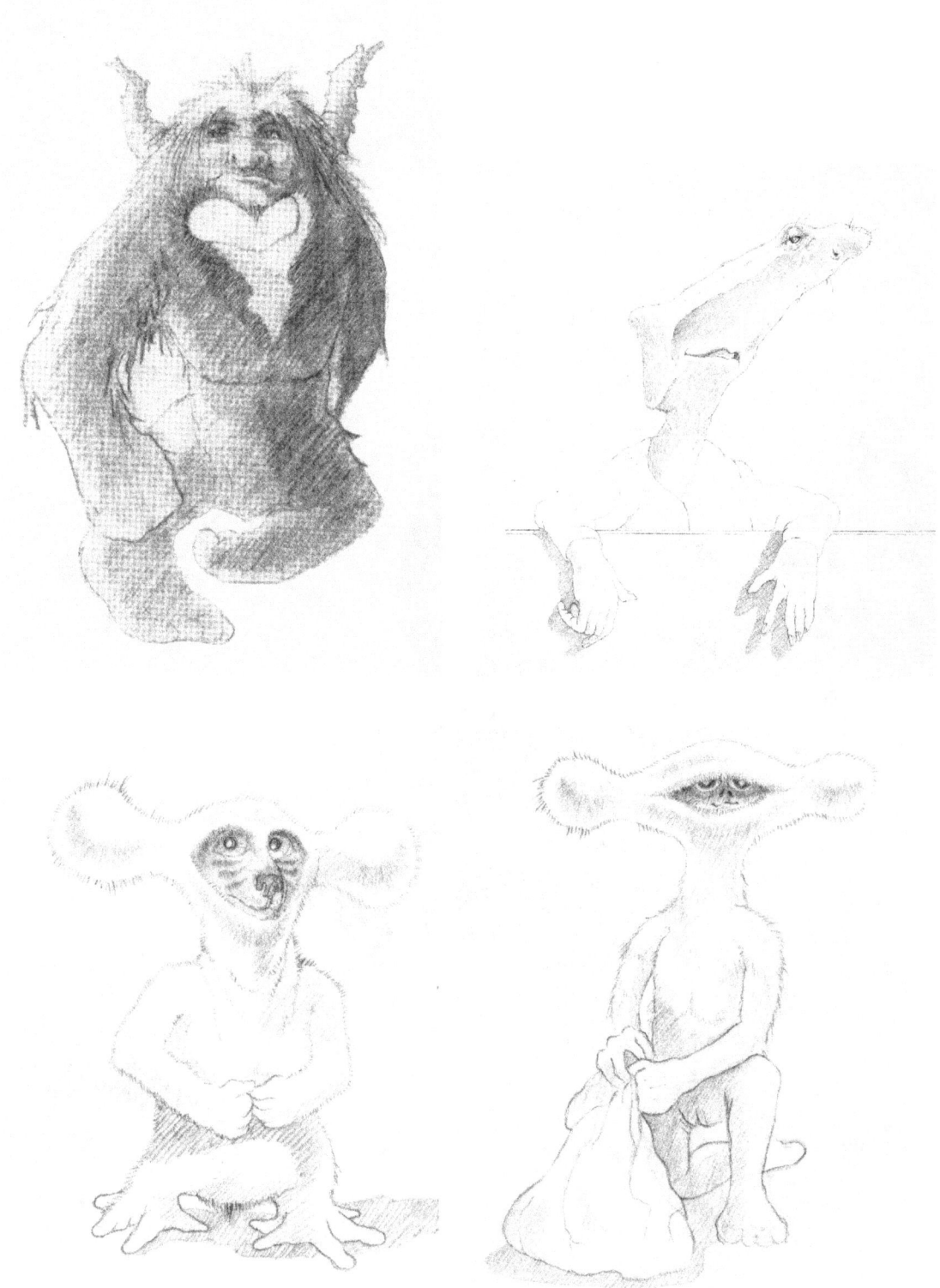

Some of the refuge hands (bottom right is a geedie… rest are not in story)

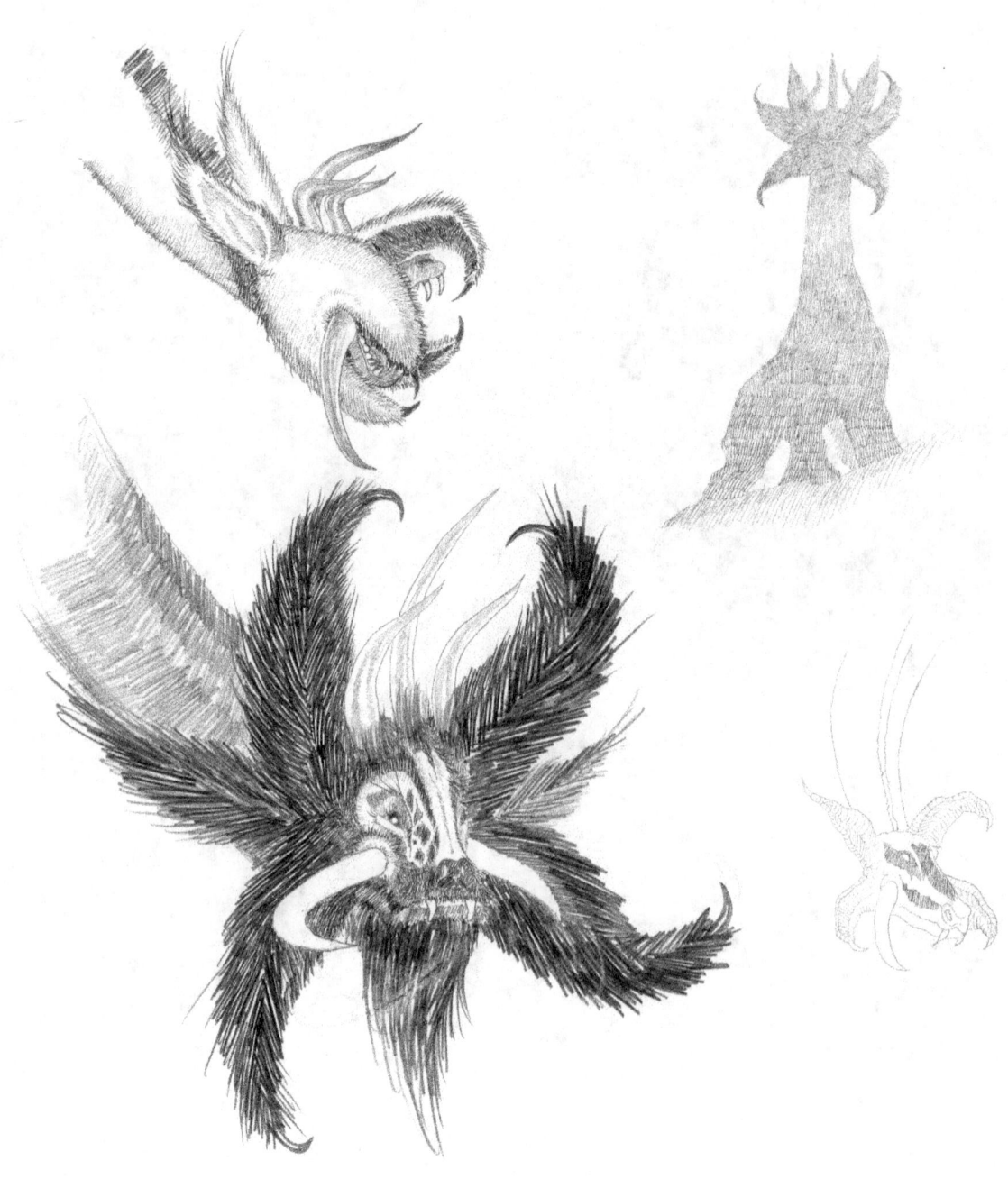

a male/bull rhontor in various poses

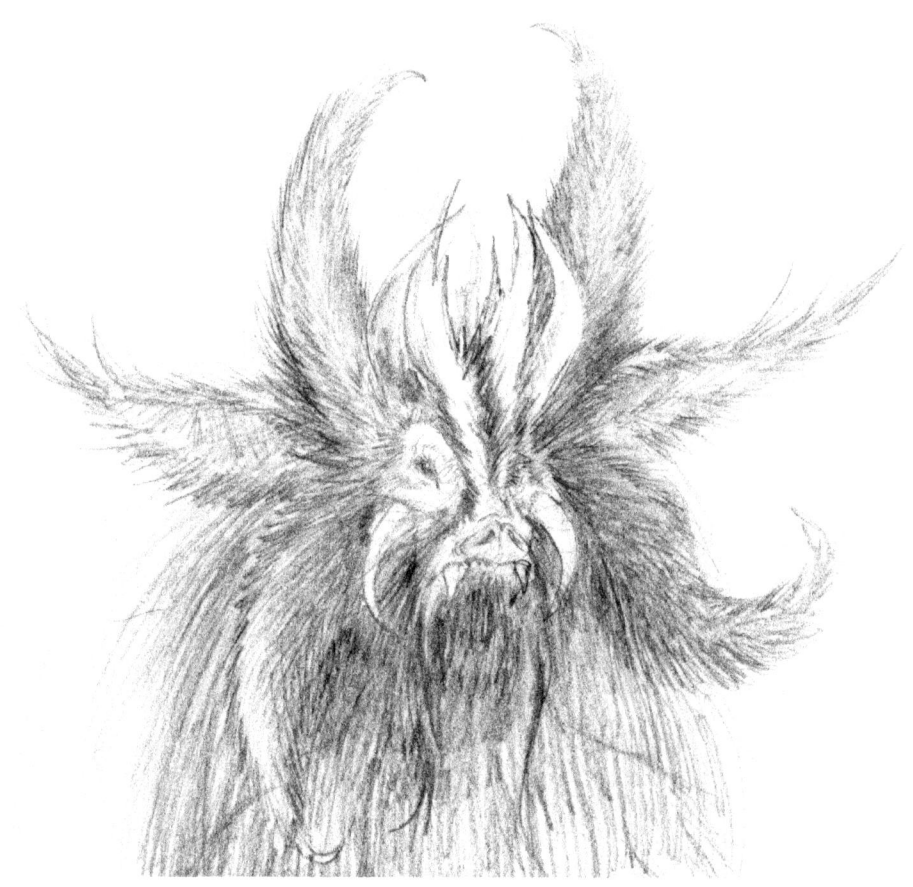

Close up of male/bull rhontor

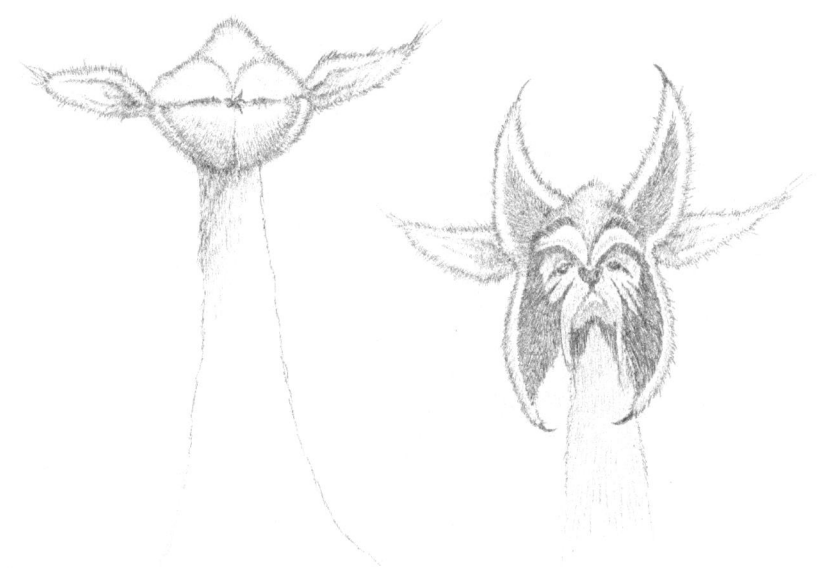

a young female rhontor

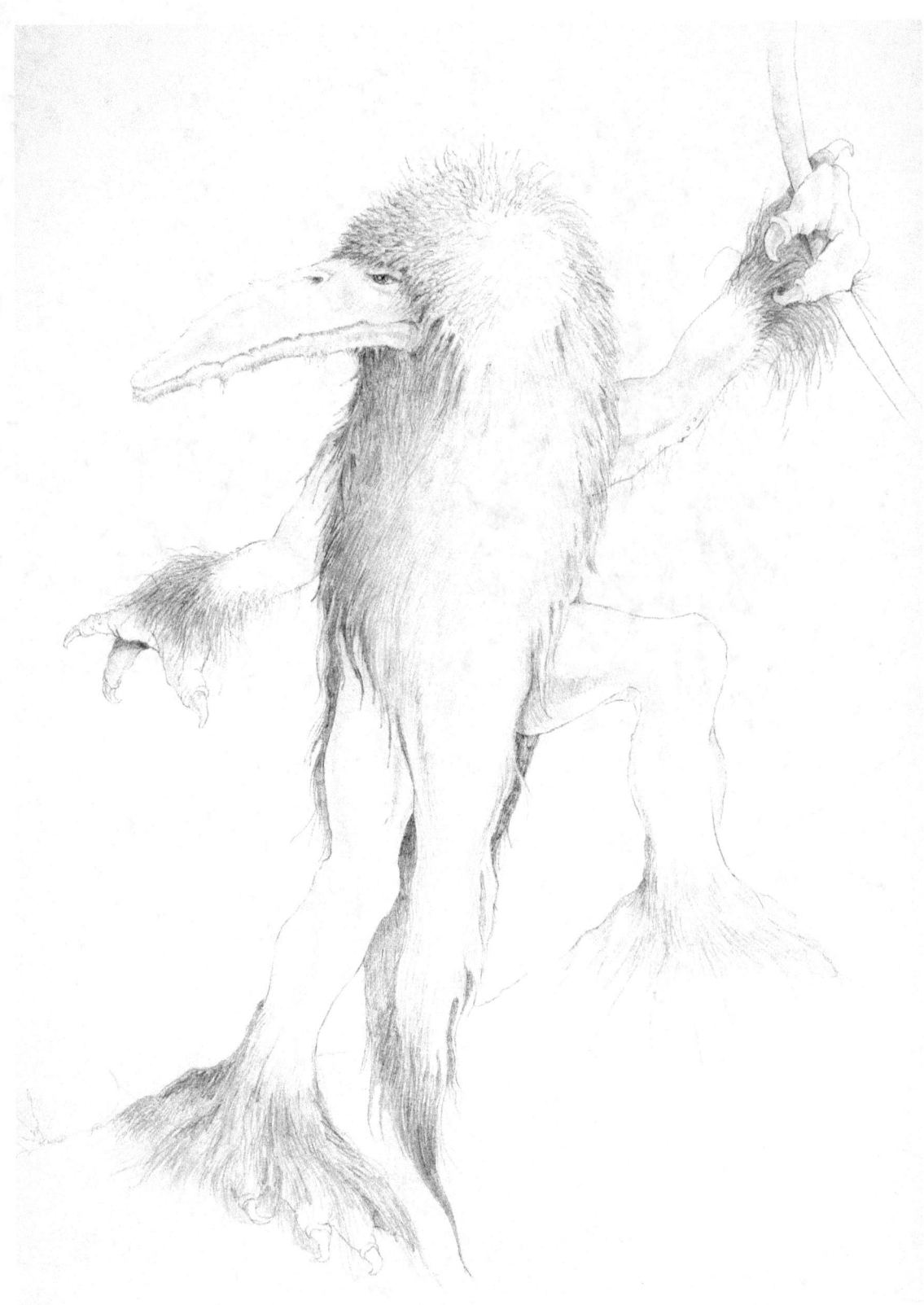

the bull goor

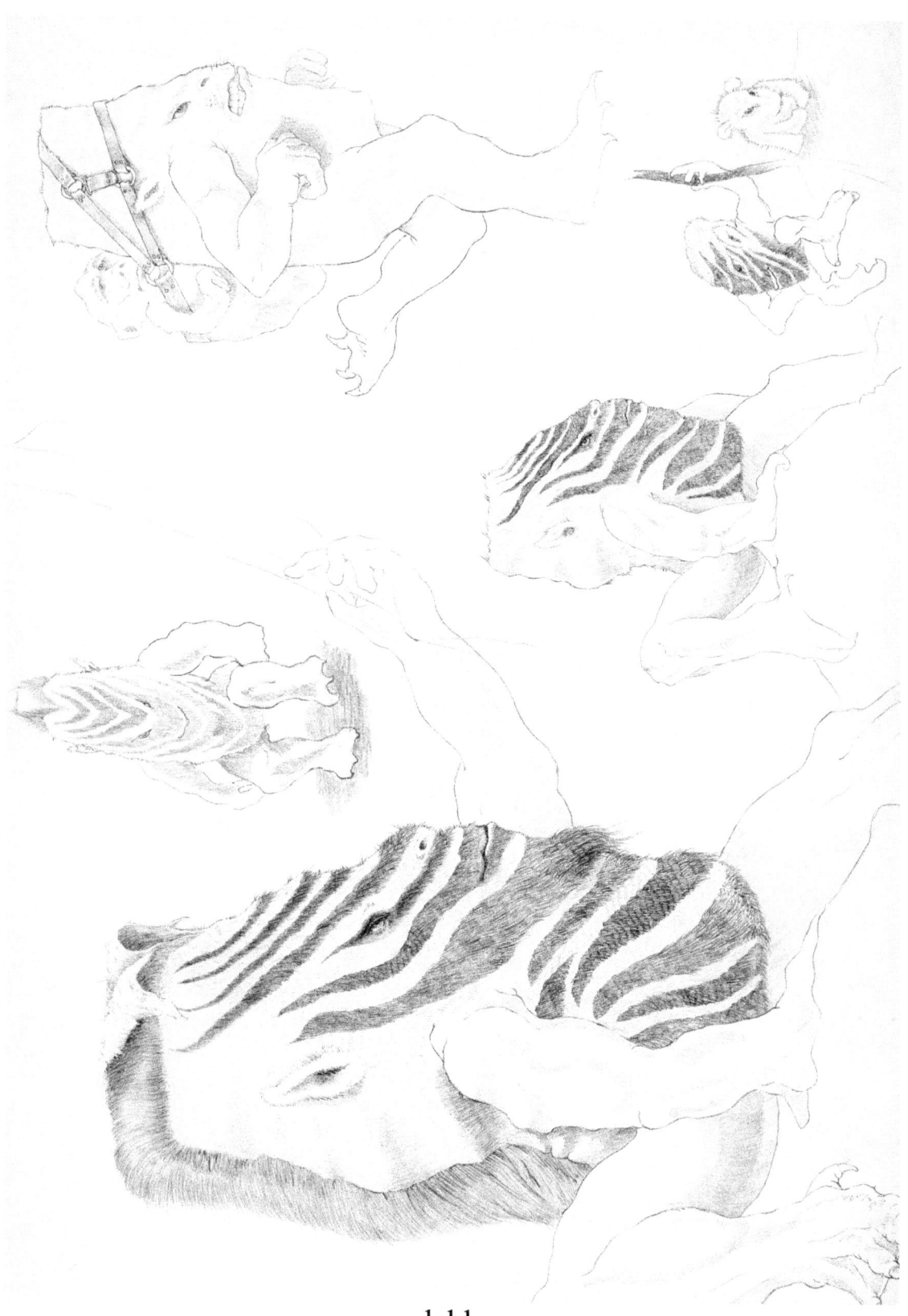

dakks

(**left to right**: bull side view, front view, female, albino top right and young ones bottom right)

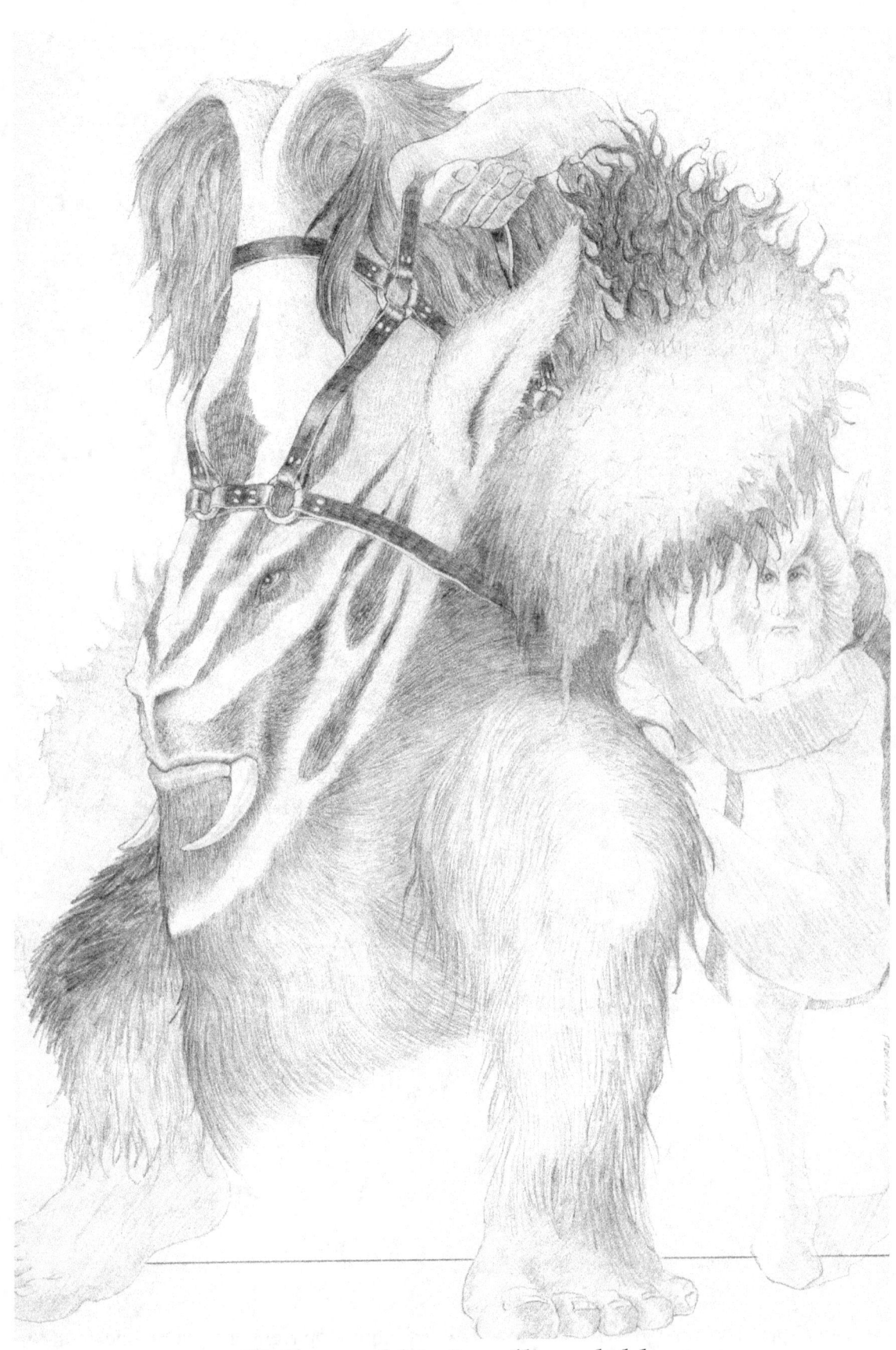

Kelbo and his Jouellian dakk

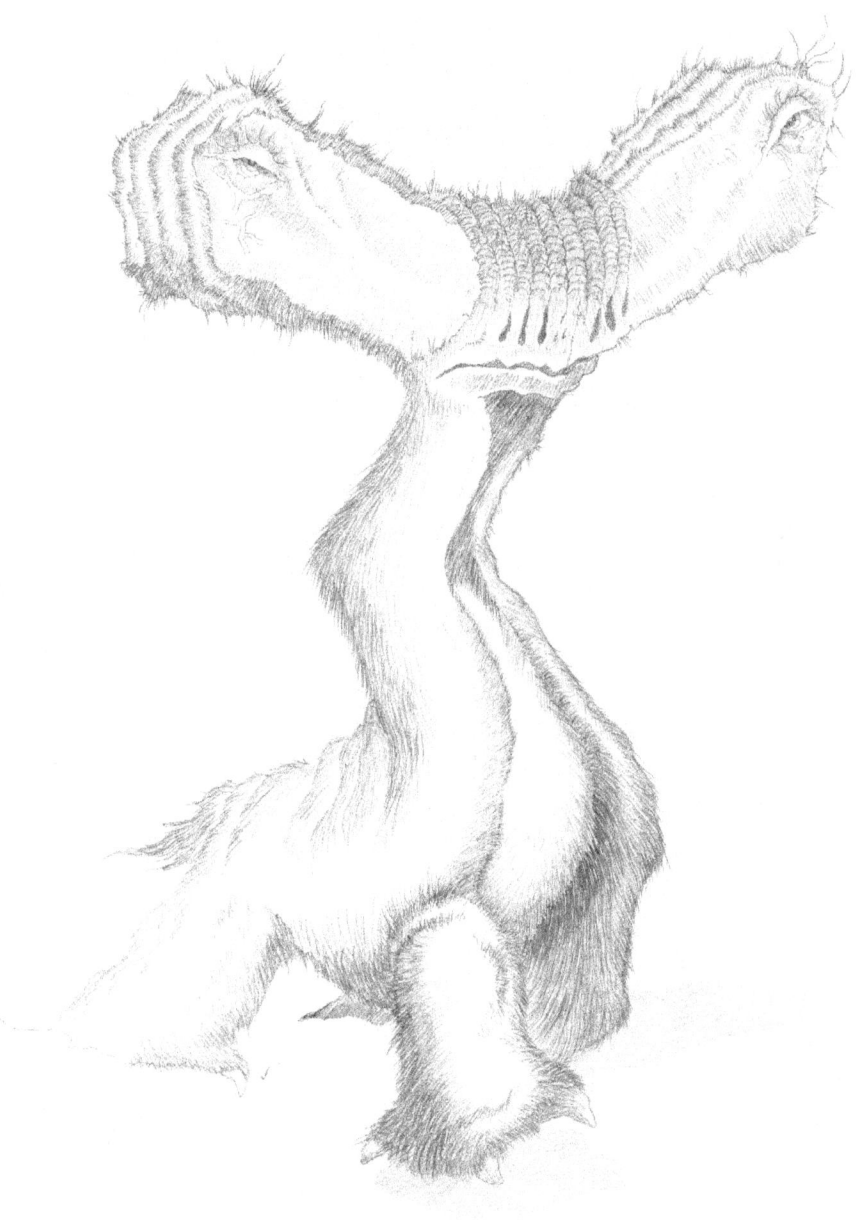

an eleud quixtor (creature on refuge not mentioned in story)

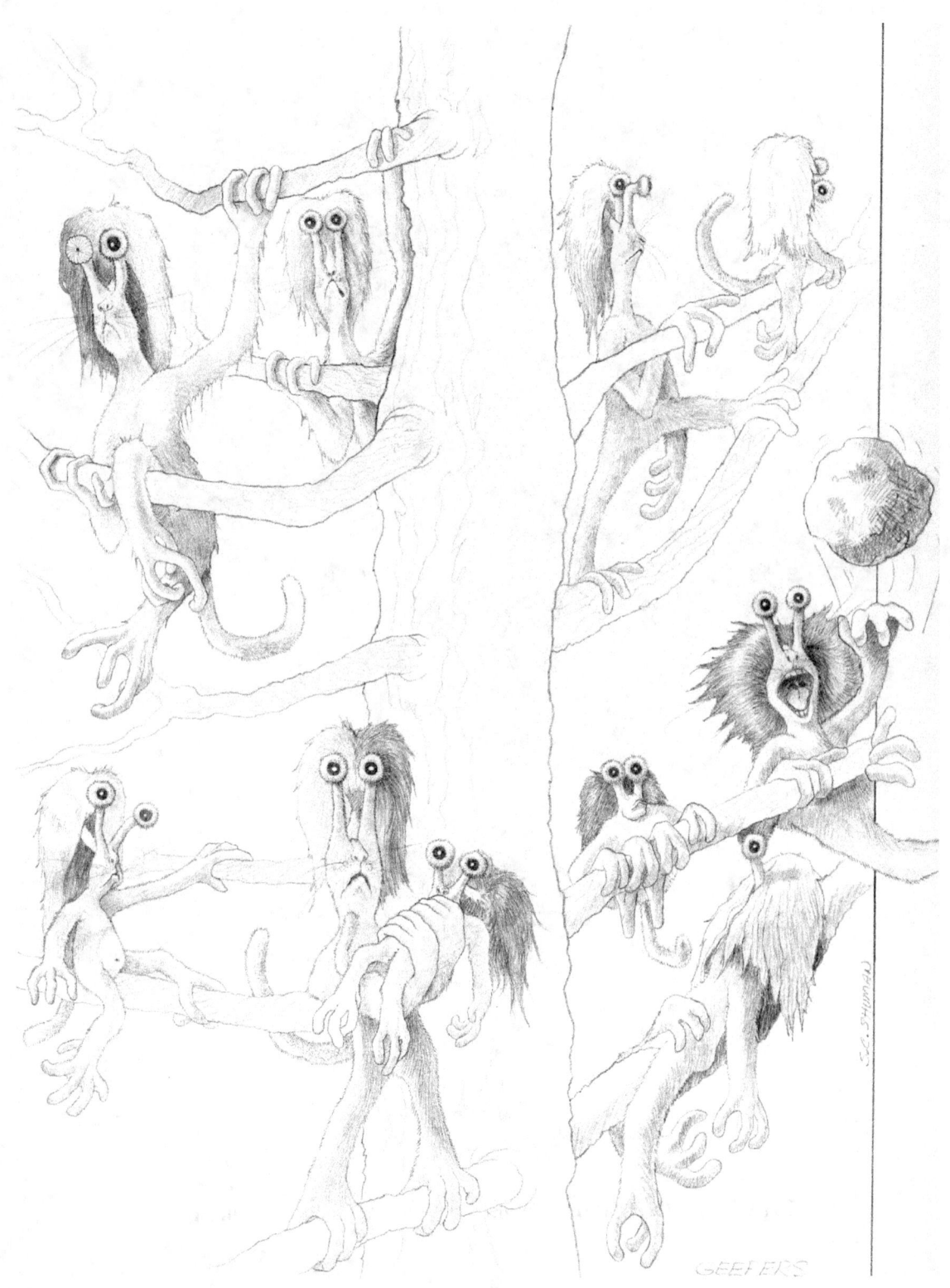

a family of geepers (creatures on refuge not mentioned in story)

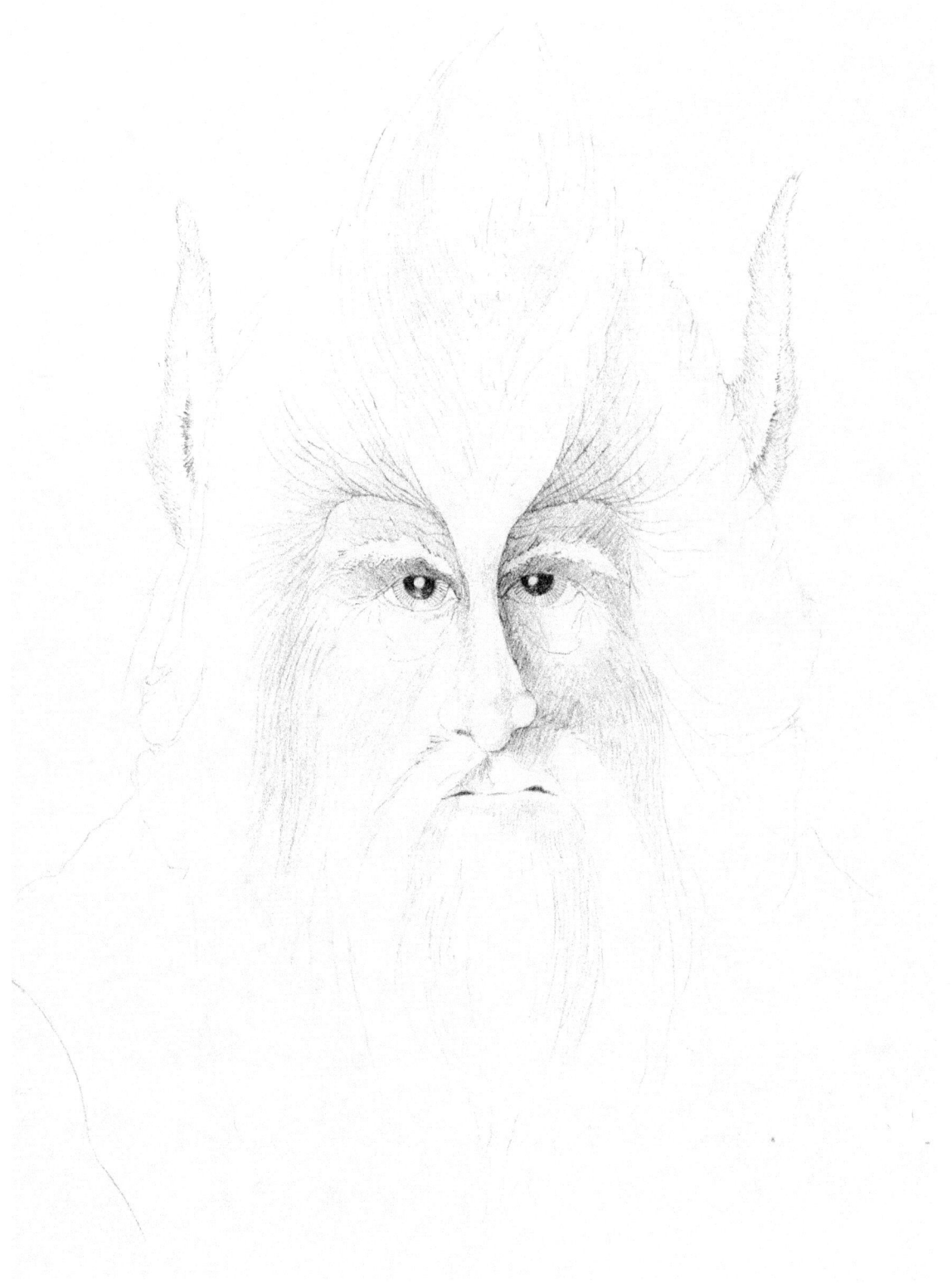

Kelbo

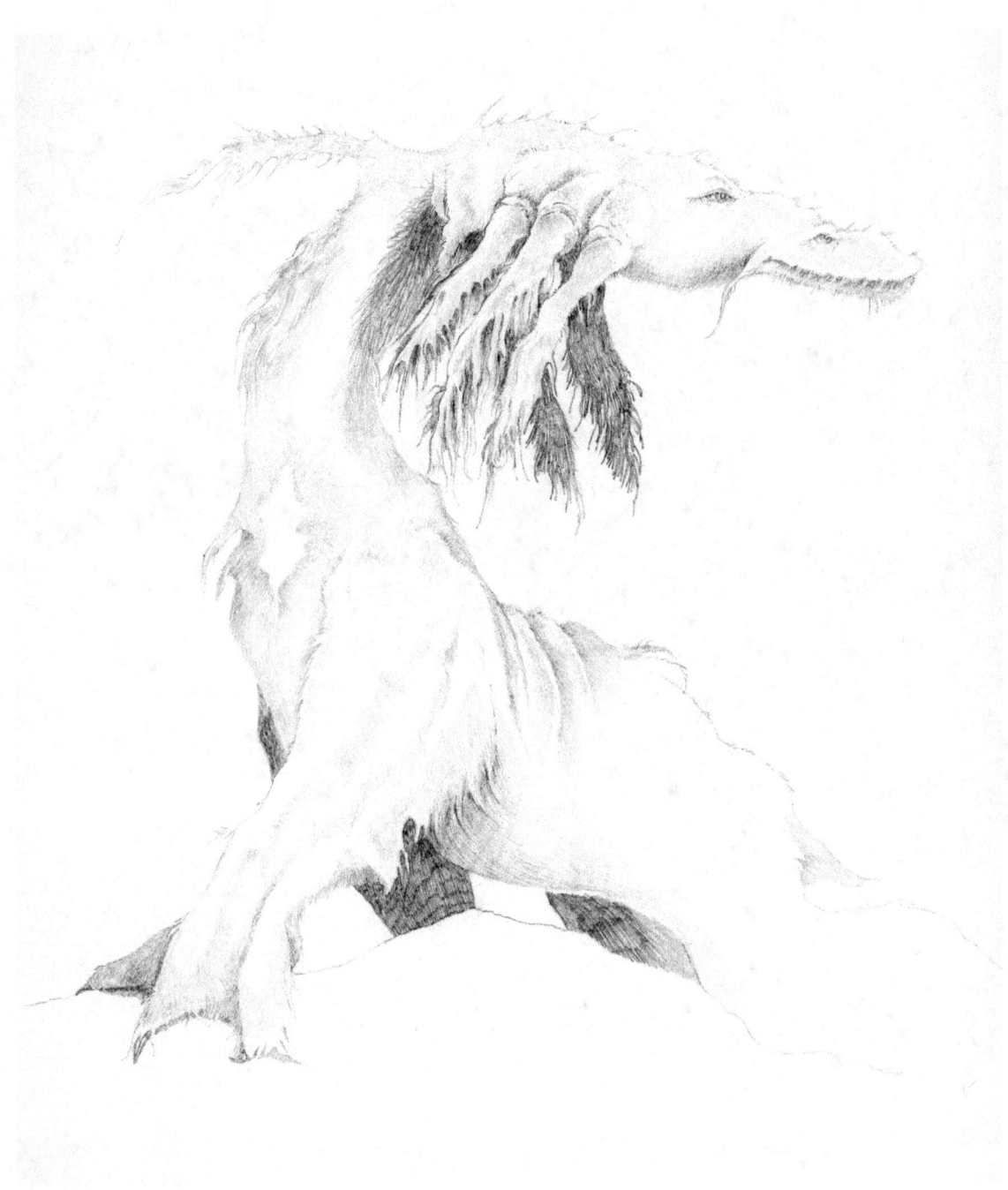

the female randa

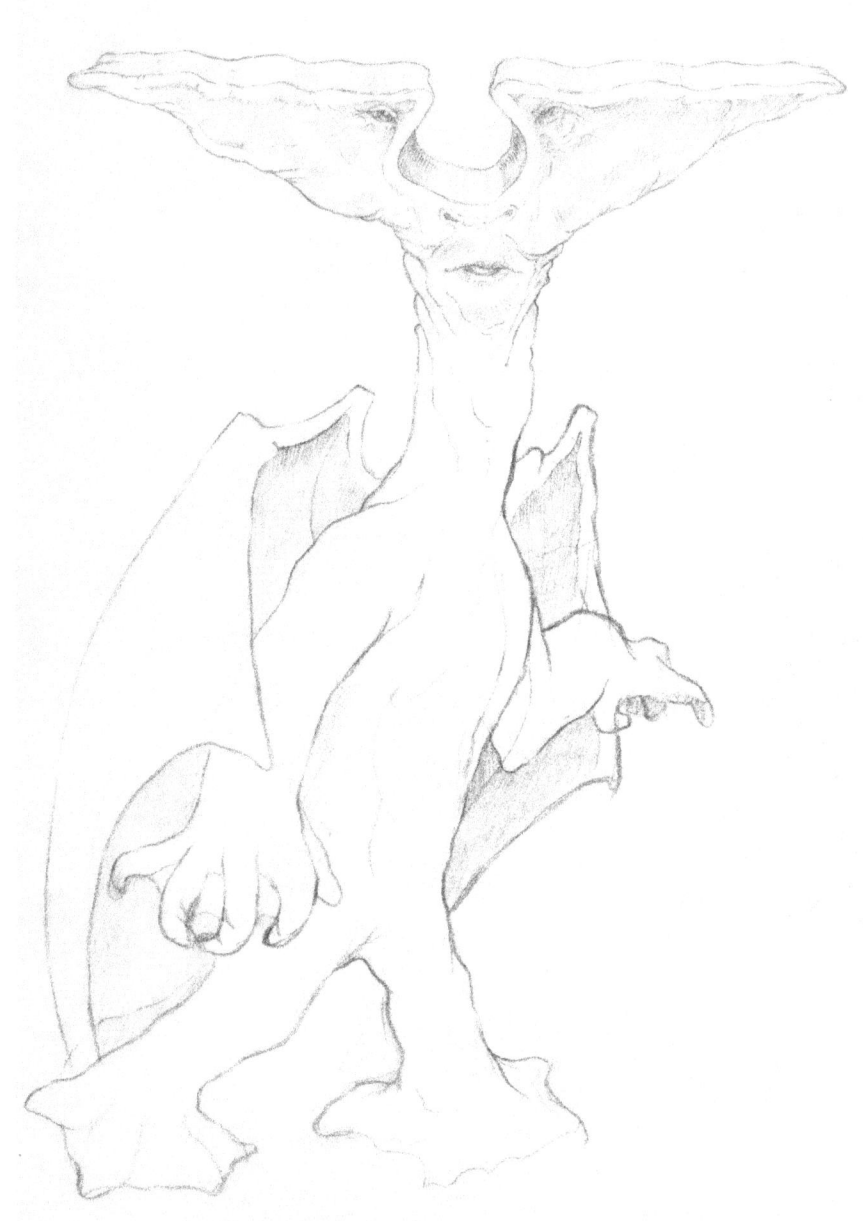

a male soarlac (a refuge creature not mentioned in story)

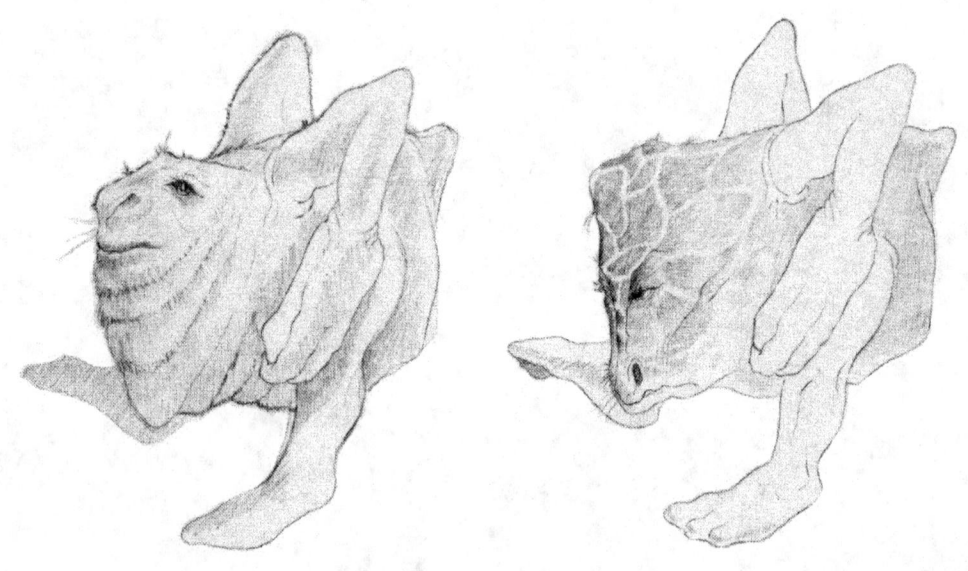

two different kinds of moargott on refuge (not mentioned in story)

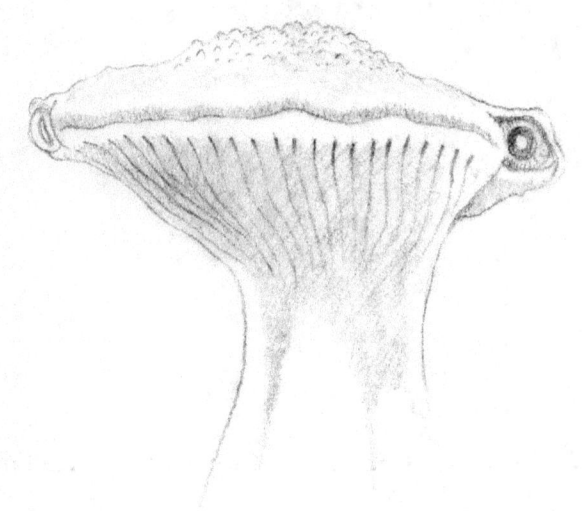

a swamp creature on refuge called a lampa (one of the creatures that did
not survive the Delcery Faucord's campaign of destruction on refuge)

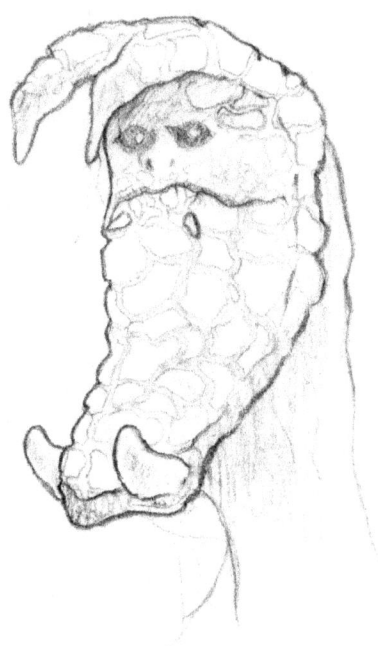

a male faalsonk (another refuge creature not mentioned in story)

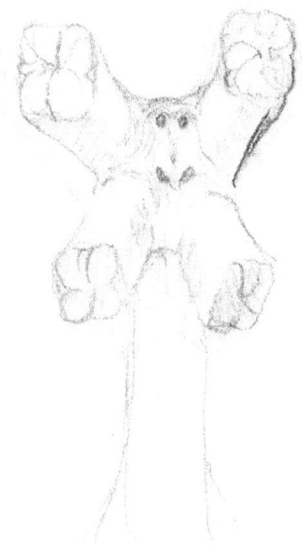

a rarely seen creature on refuge called a loorsam

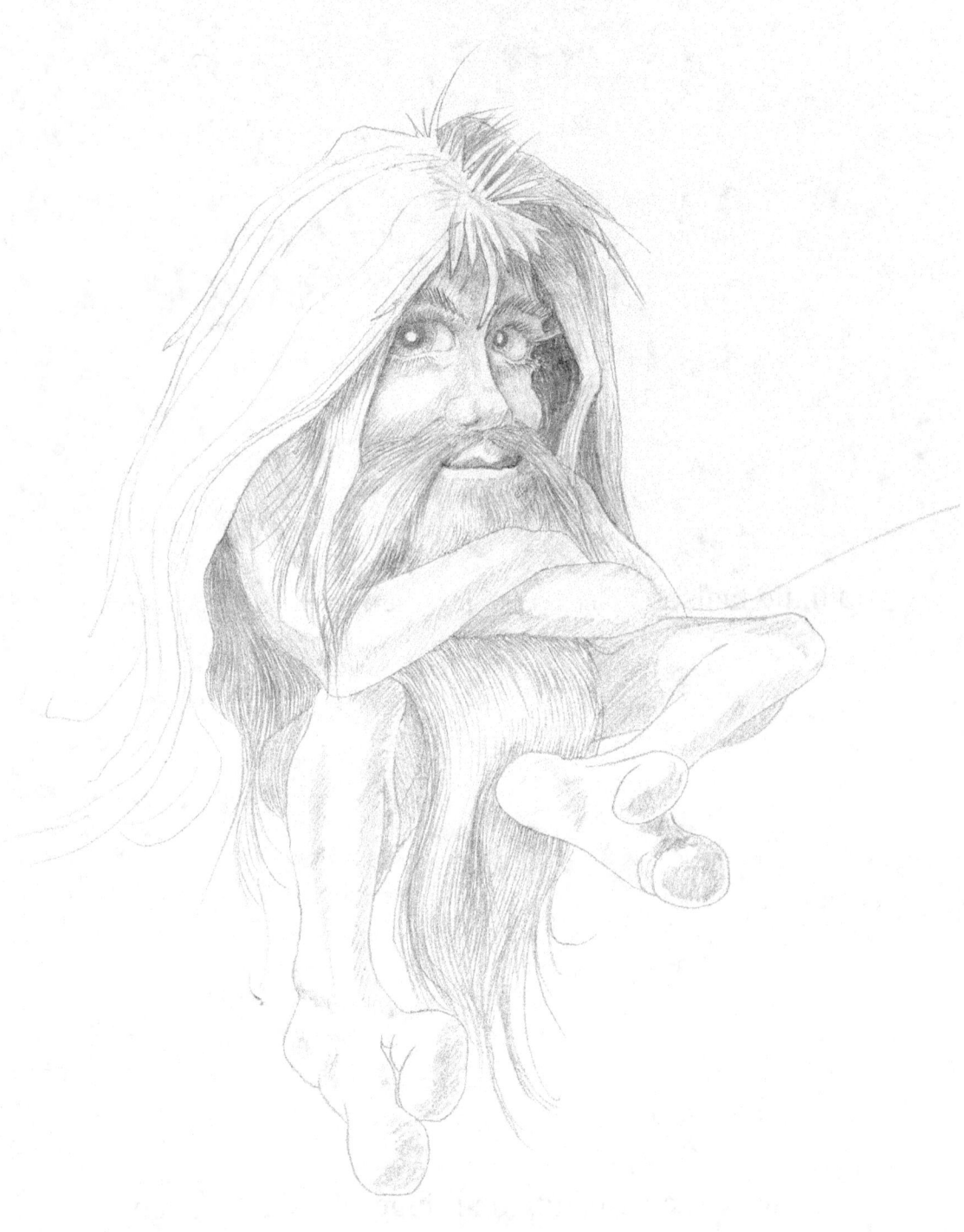

Speeb

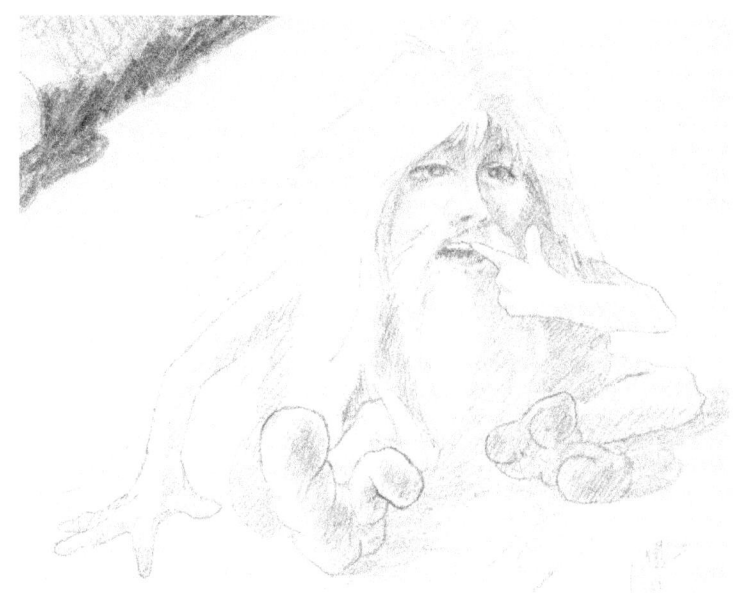

Speeb's brother Leeger (not in story)

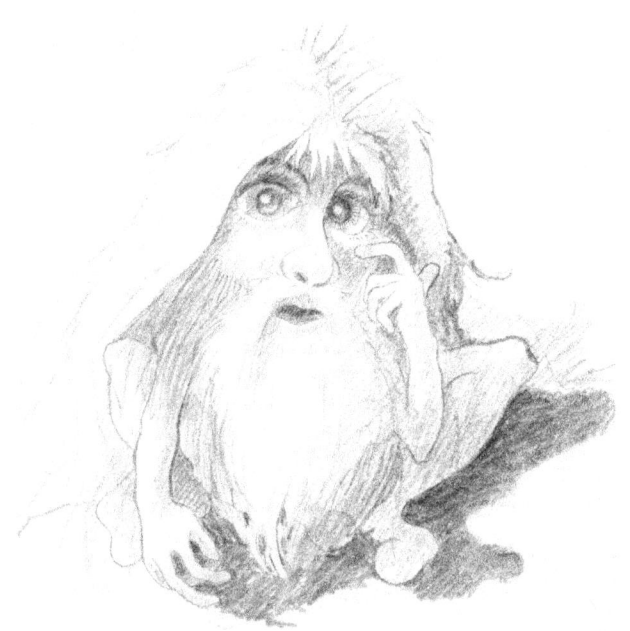

Speeb's little sister Mally (not in story)

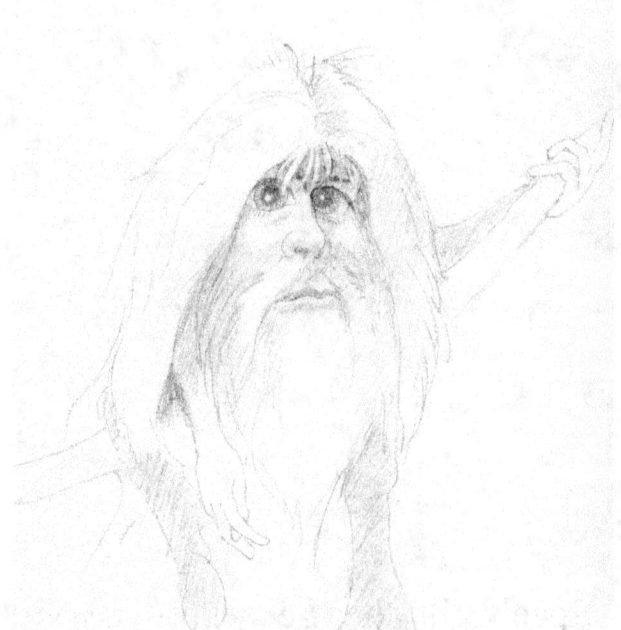

Speeb's mother (not in story)

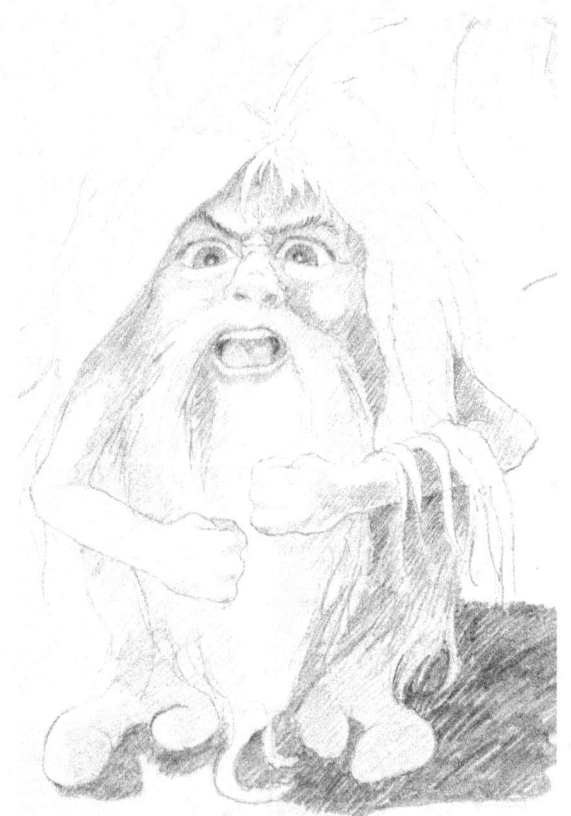

Speeb's father (not in story)

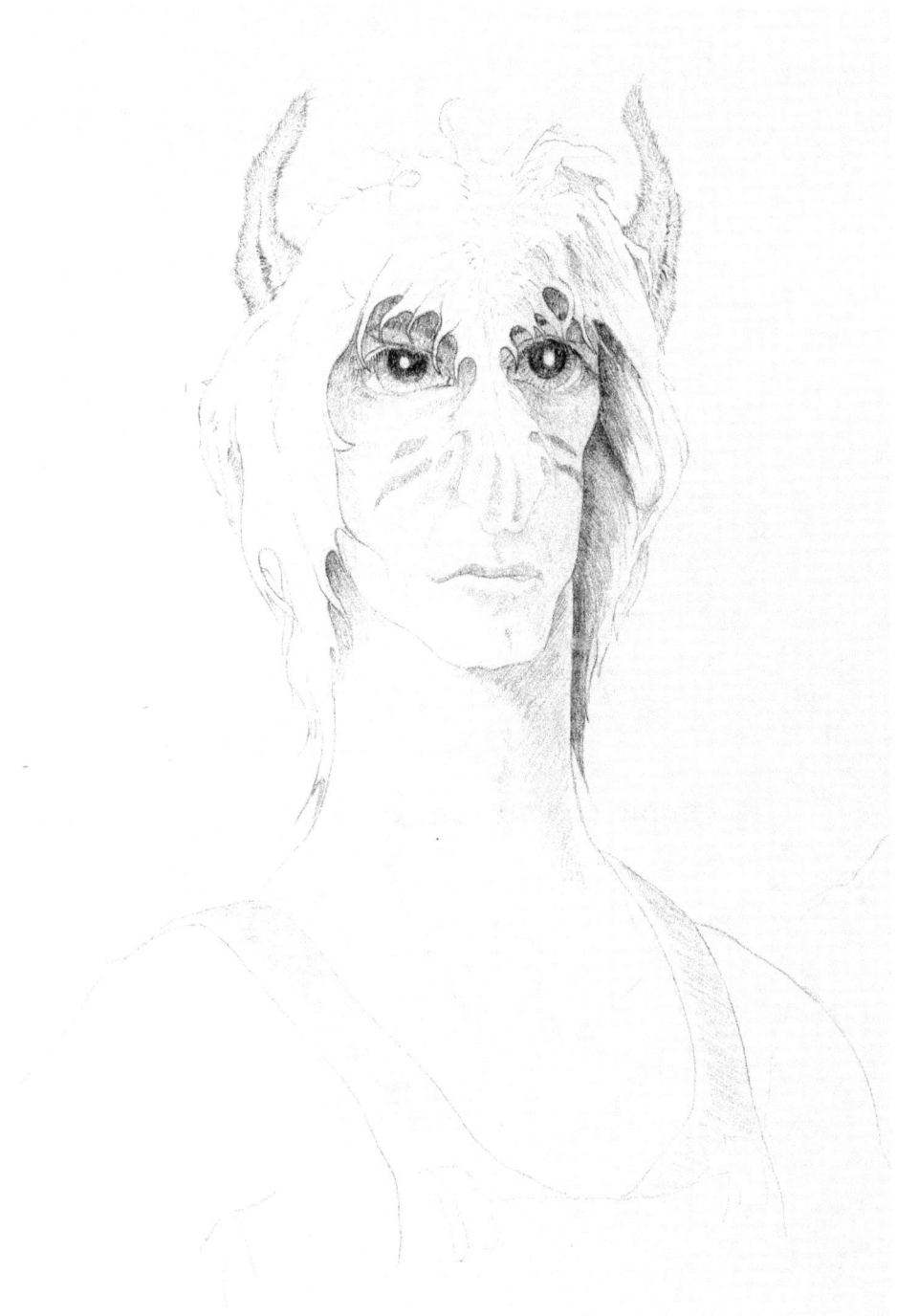

Tagg, Derol's brother

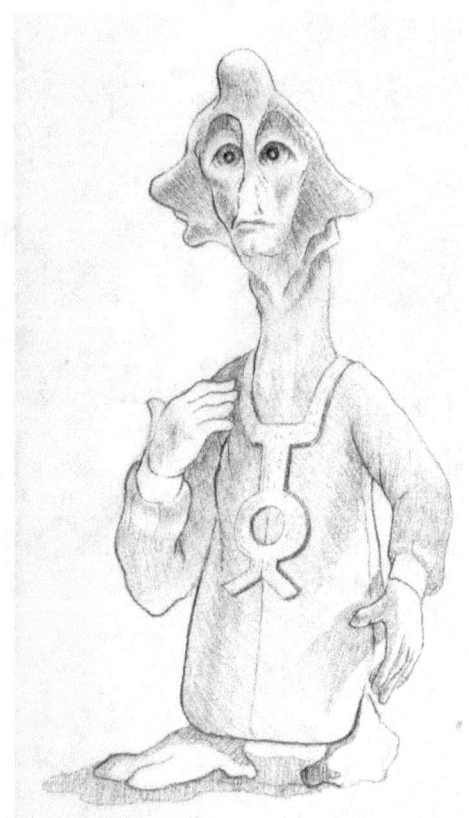

temple acolyte (not mentioned in story)

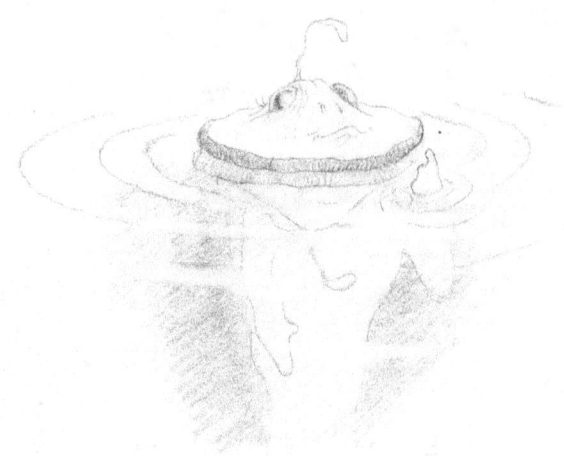

refuge creature called a water dool (not mentioned in story)

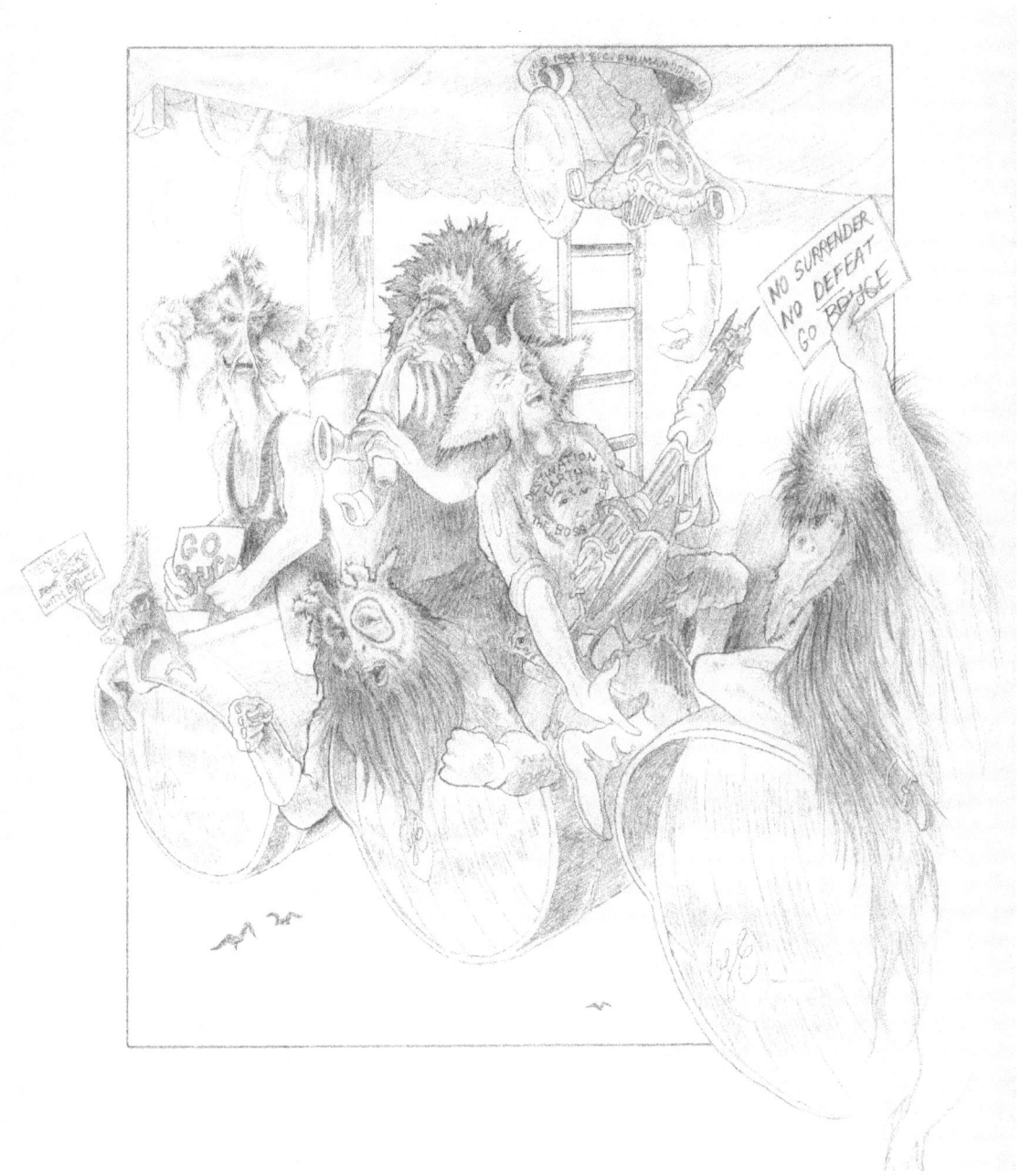

Quite a long time before the story starts, some of Derol's older brother Tagg's rowdy friends (including a tame goor!) decided to pay an unauthorized visit to Earth. They barely survived it. Little did they know that amongst their number were some future members of the Delcery Faucord.